W9-CZB-514

S. FRANCIS OF ASSISI

Leonard von Matt

THE MOST ANCIENT PORTRAIT OF THE SAINT

Painted in 1228, two years after his death, on the wall of a side-chapel at the Sacro Speco at Subiaco

S. FRANCIS
OF ASSISI

*His Life and Writings as recorded
by his contemporaries*

A new version of *The Mirror of Perfection* together with a
complete collection of all the known writings of the Saint

Translated by
LEO SHERLEY-PRICE

LONDON
A. R. MOWBRAY & Co. LIMITED

Nihil obstat: RICHARDUS ROCHE, D.D., *Censor Deputatus*
Imprimatur: ✠ FRANCISCUS, *Archiepiscopus Birmingamiensis*
Datum Birmingamiae, 15a Maii, 1959

First published in 1959

PRINTED IN GREAT BRITAIN BY
A. R. MOWBRAY & CO. LIMITED IN THE CITY OF OXFORD
8711

TRANSLATOR'S FOREWORD

THE seraphic spirit of Saint Francis of Assisi went to its reward seven hundred years ago, but the life and character of the Poverello continue to exercise a profound and beneficent influence to this day, not only among his fellow Christians but even among many who stand outside the fold of the Catholic Church. The colour and charm of his personality, his serene faith and simplicity, his love and compassion for all creatures, his gaiety and courage in suffering have touched and stirred the hearts of countless thousands. But these admirable qualities should never be viewed through a cloud of sentimentality or regarded as the sum total of his life and message, for they are only outward and visible expressions of a spiritual genius aflame with the love of God, and stem from his heroic vocation as a true servant of his Master and a loyal follower of His perfect Gospel. As with all the Saints, the secret of Saint Francis's life lies in his total abandonment to the will of God, and those who see him only as a lover of birds, beasts, and beggars miss the true significance of his character and purpose. His ministry to the lepers, his loyalty to Lady Poverty, his preaching and penitence, his courteous service of all men, his every outward activity can be understood only in relation to his hidden life of prayer, penance, and self-discipline, his literal acceptance of the Gospel way of life, and his constant recollection of the Passion of our Lord Jesus Christ, the price and means of human redemption. He was *hid with Christ in God*, so that the strength and inspiration for his exterior life sprang from his whole-hearted and self-effacing devotion to Christ Crucified, through which his unique personality and natural gifts were ever-increasingly transformed, enriched, and directed to such a degree of perfection that with

5

Saint Paul he might rightly say, *I live, yet not I, for Christ liveth in me.* The abiding attraction of Saint Francis is due, therefore, not only that of a lovable personality, but of a radiant holiness, and those who desire to understand him and share his secret of his life can best begin by reading his own writings and the true accounts given of him by his early companions.

In his *Sources for the Life of Saint Francis* Dr. J. R. H. Moorman writes: 'It is hard to understand that when Paul Sabatier wrote his famous *Vie de S. François* in 1894, the *Mirror of Perfection* was still undiscovered, although some of the chapters in it were known from a collection entitled *Speculum Vitae* and published in 1504.' Since its discovery a great deal of research has taken place, and there has been wide discussion as to its origin and value. While the subject is too complex to be of great interest to the average reader, it is important to realize that in the *Mirror of Perfection* we have much material on the life of Saint Francis which is of very early date and first-hand authority. The general consensus of opinion among Franciscan scholars is that the work was compiled at the Porziuncula about the year 1318 by an unknown member of the Order, who in one manuscript of the book states that he had drawn upon material written by the first companions of the Saint. Internal evidence reveals that this includes Thomas de Celano's *Vita Secunda* and a work known as *Legenda antiqua de Perugia* which was compiled about 1312 and was based upon the *rotuli* or parchments written by Brother Leo, the closest companion of Saint Francis, and which he is known to have deposited for safe keeping with the Sisters of Saint Clare, at San Damiano. These parchments, now lost, contained Leo's personal reminiscences and stories of his friend and Master. In those days it was quite customary for a writer to adapt or transcribe material from the works of others without making any formal acknowledgement, and it is virtually certain that although the *Mirror* cannot be ascribed to Brother Leo himself, it rests largely on his authority and contains a great deal of material lifted bodily from his writings, together with other

6

material sent in to Assisi by other individuals or groups of friars in response to an appeal by Crescentius, Minister-General of the Order, in 1244.

From the outset it will be apparent to the reader that the *Mirror of Perfection* is not intended to provide a full and chronological biography of Saint Francis; this had already been attempted with limited success both by Thomas of Celano, who had been entrusted with this task by Pope Gregory IX, and by Saint Bonaventura, Minister-General of the Order. Rather is it a rosary of stories linked together by the chain of Saint Francis's personality, and selected so as to illustrate various aspects of his life and mission to the world. Accordingly these accounts are grouped together under such headings as 'His perfect poverty,' 'His love for created things,' 'His zeal for prayer,' so that the reader may understand, ponder, and emulate the real qualities of the Little Poor Man of Assisi, the Pattern of the Friars and the Mirror of Perfection for all who seek to walk in the way of the Gospel.

May the inspiration of his life and the support of his prayers strengthen those who read this book, and enable them to conquer the temptations, problems, and fears of this present age in the spirit and power of Christ.

LEO SHERLEY-PRICE

ACKNOWLEDGEMENTS

As it seems appropriate that a modern translation of the life and writings of S. Francis should be accompanied by a modern translation of the Vulgate, all quotations from Holy Scripture in this work are taken from the version by the late Monsignor Ronald Knox, by permission of the Cardinal Archbishop of Westminster and of Messrs. Burns Oates & Washbourne Ltd., publishers.

The illustrations are reproduced from photographs taken by Leonard von Matt, Buochs, Switzerland, by kind permission.

CONTENTS

THE MIRROR OF PERFECTION

THE WRITINGS OF S. FRANCIS

ILLUSTRATIONS

THE MIRROR OF PERFECTION

1

PROLOGUE

S. Francis's reply to the Ministers who were unwilling to obey the Rule.

AFTER the second Rule written by blessed Francis had been lost, he went up a mountain (*Monte Colombo, near Rieti*) with Brother Leo of Assisi and Brother Bonizo of Bologna, to draw up another, and under the guidance of Christ he had it written down. But many Ministers came in a body to Brother Elias, the Vicar of blessed Francis, and said, 'We hear that Brother Francis is drawing up a new Rule, and we fear that he will make it so harsh that it will be impossible for us to keep it. So we would like you to go and tell him that we are not willing to be bound by this Rule. Let him make it for himself, and not for us.' But Brother Elias feared a rebuke from the holy Father, and refused to go. And when they all pressed him, he said that he would not go without them, so they all went together.

When Brother Elias approached the place where blessed Francis was standing, he called to him. And when he had answered and saw the Ministers, he asked, 'What do these Brothers want?' Brother Elias said, 'They are Ministers, who hear that you are drawing up a new Rule, and they fear that you intend to make it too harsh. They refuse to be bound by it, and ask you to make it for yourself, and not for them.'

At this blessed Francis raised his face to heaven and spoke to Christ, saying, 'Lord, was I not right when I said that they would not believe me?' And all present heard the voice of Christ answer from heaven, 'Francis, nothing in this Rule is yours; for all is Mine. I wish the Rule to be obeyed to the letter, to the letter, without a gloss, without a gloss. I know what the frailty of man can achieve, and I know how much I intend to help them. So let those who are not willing to obey the Rule leave the Order.'

Then blessed Francis turned to the friars and said, 'You have heard! You have heard! Do you want this to be repeated?' And the Ministers confessed their fault and went away confused and terrified.

Part I

ON THE PERFECTION OF POVERTY

2

*Firstly, how blessed Francis made known his will and intention (which
he maintained from beginning to end) with regard to the observance of
poverty.*

FRIAR Richard of the March was a man of noble birth, but even
more noble in his holiness, and blessed Francis loved him dearly.
One day he visited blessed Francis in the palace of the Bishop
of Assisi, and among other matters that they discussed relating
to the Order and the observance of the Rule, he asked him
particularly on the following, saying, 'Tell me, Father, what
was your original intention when you began to have brethren?
And what is it to-day? And do you intend to maintain it to
the day of your death? If I know this, I shall be able to testify
to your intention and will from first to last. For example, may
we friars who are clergy and possess many books keep them,
provided that we regard them as the property of the Order?'

Blessed Francis said to him, 'I assure you, brother, that it has
been and remains my first and last intention and desire—had
the brethren only believed me—that no friar should possess anything but a habit, a cord, and an undergarment, as our Rule
allows.'

But if any friar should be inclined to ask, 'Why did not blessed
Francis insist that poverty was observed by the friars in his own
day, as he told Brother Richard? And why did he not enforce
its observance?', we who were with him can answer this question
as we have heard it from his own mouth, for he himself spoke
to the friars on this and on many other matters. For the guidance
of the Order he also caused many things which he had learned

from God by constant prayer and meditation, to be written in the Rule, declaring them to be in accordance with God's will. But after he had revealed these things to the friars, they thought them harsh and unbearable, for they did not know what was to happen in the Order after his death.

And because he feared dissension between himself and the friars, he was not willing to argue with them, but reluctantly yielded to their wishes, and asked pardon of God. But in order that the words which the Lord had put into his mouth for the guidance of the friars should not pass unheeded, he resolved to observe them himself, and by so doing to obtain his reward from God. At length he found contentment in this, and his soul received comfort.

3

Saint Francis's reply to a Minister who asked his permission to have books; and how the Ministers removed the chapter containing the Gospel prohibitions from the Rule without his knowledge.

ONCE, when blessed Francis had returned from overseas, one of the Ministers was discussing the chapter on poverty with him, wishing in particular to learn his own will and interpretation of it; especially since at that time the Rule contained a chapter on the prohibitions of the Gospel, namely, *Take nothing with you on the journey, etc.*

And blessed Francis answered him, 'My intention is that the friars should possess nothing but a habit, with a cord and undergarment, as the Rule requires. And anyone who is compelled by necessity may wear sandals.'

The Minister said, 'What shall I do, for I have books worth more than fifty pounds?' He said this because he wished to have them with a clear conscience, and knowing how strictly blessed Francis interpreted the chapter on poverty, it troubled him to possess so many books.

Blessed Francis said to him, 'I will not, should not, and cannot go against my own conscience and the perfection of the holy Gospel which we have vowed to observe.' Hearing this, the Minister was grieved; but seeing him so disturbed, blessed Francis said to him with great fervour of spirit in the presence of all the friars, 'You wish people to recognize you as Friars Minor, and to regard you as men who observe the holy Gospel; yet you want to have chests for your books!'

But although the Ministers knew that the friars were obliged to observe the holy Gospel according to the Rule, they removed from the Rule the chapter where it is said, *Take nothing for your journey*, and thought that by so doing they would not be bound to observe the perfection of the Gospel. This was revealed to blessed Francis by the Holy Spirit, and he said in the presence of certain friars, 'The Friar Ministers think they can deceive God and me. On the contrary, in order that all friars shall know themselves bound to observe the perfection of the Gospel, I wish it to be written at the beginning and at the end of the Rule that friars are bound to the strict observance of the Holy Gospel of our Lord Jesus Christ. And in order that the brethren may never have any excuse to set aside the things that I have proclaimed and still proclaim, which the Lord has placed in my mouth for their salvation and my own, I intend to demonstrate these things before God by my own actions, and by His help, I will observe them for ever.'

So, from the early days when he began to have brethren to the day of his death, blessed Francis observed the whole of the Gospel to the letter.

4

On the novice who sought his permission to own a psalter.

AT another time a friar novice who knew how to recite the psalter, although not fluently, obtained leave from the Minister

General to have his own copy. But having heard that blessed Francis did not wish his friars to hanker after learning and books, he was not happy about having it without his permission. So when blessed Francis was visiting the friary to which this novice belonged, the novice said to him, 'Father, it would give me great pleasure to have a psalter. But although the Minister General has granted permission, I would like to have it with your approval.' To which blessed Francis replied, 'The Emperor Charles, Roland, Oliver, and all the paladins and men of valour were mighty in battle, fought the Infidels until death with great sweat and toil, and they gained a famous victory. And the holy martyrs themselves gave their lives in battle for the Faith of Christ. But in these days there are many who wish to win honour and praise from men by merely telling of their deeds. In the same way, there are many among us who want to win honour and praise by merely proclaiming and reciting the deeds of the Saints.' As though to say, 'Our concern is not with books and learning, but with holy deeds; for learning brings pride, but charity edifies.'

Some days later, as blessed Francis was sitting by the fire, the novice spoke to him again about the psalter. And blessed Francis said to him, 'Once you have a psalter, you will want a breviary. And when you have a breviary, you will sit in a high chair like a great prelate, and say to your brother, "Bring me my breviary!"' As he spoke, blessed Francis in great fervour of spirit took up a handful of ashes and placed them on his head, and rubbing his hand around his head as though he was washing it, he exclaimed, 'I, a breviary! I, a breviary!' And he repeated this many times, passing his hand over his head. And the friar was amazed and ashamed.

Later, blessed Francis said to him, 'Brother, I was tempted in the same way to have books, but in order to learn the will of our Lord in this matter, I took the Gospels and prayed the Lord to reveal His will to me at the first opening of the book. And when my prayer was ended, at the first opening of the book

I came upon the words of the holy Gospel, *It is granted to you to understand the secret of God's kingdom; the rest must learn of it by parables.'* And he said, 'There are so many who are eager to acquire learning, that blessed is the man who is content to be without it for love of the Lord God.'

Many months later, when blessed Francis was at S. Mary of the Porziuncula, this friar spoke to him yet again about the psalter as he stood on the road near his cell beyond the house. And blessed Francis told him, 'Go and do as your Minister says on this matter.' When he heard this, the friar turned back along the road, while blessed Francis stood thinking over what he had said to the friar. Suddenly he called after him, saying, 'Wait for me, brother, wait for me!' Overtaking him, he said, 'Come back and show me the place where I told you to do as your Minister directs about the psalter.' So when they had arrived at the place, blessed Francis knelt down before the friar and said, '*Mea culpa*, brother, *mea culpa*; for whoever wishes to be a Friar Minor should possess nothing but a habit with a cord and undergarment, as the Rule allows him. And those whom need obliges to do so may have sandals.' And whenever friars came to him to ask his advice on this matter, he used to give them the same reply. He often used to say, 'A man's knowledge is revealed by his actions, and the words of a Religious must be supported by his own deeds; for *the test of the tree is in its fruit.'*

5

On observing poverty in books and beds, buildings and appointments.

THE most blessed Father used to teach the friars to value books for their witness to God and not for their costliness, for their edification and not their elegance. He wished books to be few and held in common, and suitable to the needs of penniless friars. They were so badly provided with beds and blankets that whoever had some threadbare rags spread over straw regarded it as a fine bed.

He also told the friars to build their houses small and their cells of wood, not of stone, and he wanted them built in a humble style. He abhorred pretentious buildings, and disliked superfluous or elaborate appointments. He wished nothing about their tables or appointments to appear worldly or to remind them of the world, so that everything should proclaim their poverty and remind them that they were pilgrims and exiles.

6

How Saint Francis compelled all the friars to leave a house which had been called 'the house of the friars.'

WHILE he was passing through Bologna, he heard that a house had recently been built there for the friars. Directly he learned that it was known as 'the house of the friars,' he turned on his heel and left the city, giving strict orders that all the friars were to leave it at once and live in it no longer.

So they all abandoned it, and even the sick were not allowed to remain, but were turned out with the rest, until the Lord Ugolino, Bishop of Ostia and Legate in Lombardy, publicly proclaimed that the house belonged to him. One of these friars, who was sick and obliged to leave the house, is still living to-day, and has written this account.

7

How Saint Francis wished to destroy a house which the people of Assisi had built at S. Mary of the Porziuncula.

AT this period the friars had only a single poor cell thatched with straw, with walls of wattle and daub. So when the time drew near for the General Chapter, which was held each year at

S. Mary of the Porziuncula, the people of Assisi, realizing that the friars were increasing in number daily, and that all of them assembled there each year, held a meeting. And within a few days, with great haste and zeal, they erected a large building of stone and mortar while blessed Francis was absent and knew nothing of it.

When he returned from one of the Provinces and arrived for the Chapter, he was astonished at the house built there. And he was afraid that the sight of this house might make other friars build similar large houses in the places where they lived or were to live, and he desired this place to remain the example and pattern for all other houses of the Order. So before the Chapter ended he climbed onto the roof of the house and told other friars to climb up with him. And with their help he began to throw to the ground the tiles with which the house was roofed, intending to destroy it to the very foundations. But some men-at-arms of Assisi were present to protect the place from the great crowd of sightseers who had gathered to watch the Chapter of the Friars. And when they saw that blessed Francis and other friars intended to destroy the house, they went up to him at once and said, 'Brother, this house belongs to the Commune of Assisi, and we are here to represent the Commune. We forbid you to destroy our house.' When he heard this, blessed Francis said to them, 'If the house is yours, I will not touch it.' And forthwith he and the other friars came down.

As a result of this incident, the people of the City of Assisi decreed that thenceforward whoever held the office of Mayor should be responsible for the repair of the house. And each year for a long time this decree was carried out.

How he rebuked his Vicar because he was having a small house built for the recitation of the Office.

ON another occasion the Vicar of blessed Francis began to have a small house built at S. Mary's, where the friars could be quiet and recite the Hours, because so many friars visited the place that they had nowhere in which to say the Office. For all the friars of the Order used to come there, because no one was received into the Order except in S. Mary's.

When the building was nearly completed, blessed Francis returned to the friary, and while in his cell he heard the noise made by the workmen. Calling his companion, he inquired what the friars were doing, and his companion told him all that was happening.

Blessed Francis immediately sent for his Vicar, and said to him, 'Brother, this place is the example and pattern of the whole Order. I would rather have the friars living here put up with trouble and discomfort for love of the Lord God, so that other friars who come here carry away to their own houses a good example of poverty, rather than that they should enjoy every convenience and that these others should carry back to their own houses an example of building, saying, "At the friary of Saint Mary of the Porziuncula, which is the chief house of the Order, there are such and such great buildings, so we may rightly build in our own places as well." '

9

How he was not willing to remain in a well-built cell, or one that was called his own.

ONE of the friars, a deeply spiritual man, who was very intimate with blessed Francis, had a cell built standing a little distance from the hermitage where he lived, so that blessed Francis could remain at prayer there whenever he visited the place. So when blessed Francis came there, this friar conducted him to the cell; but although it was built only of wood, rough-hewn with axe and hatchet, the Father said, 'This cell is too fine. If you wish me to stay here, have a cell made with branches and ferns as its only covering inside and out.' For the poorer and smaller the house or cell, the readier he was to live in it. And when the friar had done this, blessed Francis remained there for some days.

One day, however, when he had left the cell, one of the friars went to look at it, and afterwards came to the place where blessed Francis was. Seeing him, the holy Father said to him, 'Where have you come from, brother?' 'I have come from your cell,' he replied. Then blessed Francis said, 'Because you have called it mine, some one else shall use it henceforward, and not I.' For we who were with him have often heard him quote the saying, *Foxes have holes, and the birds of the air their resting-places; the Son of Man has nowhere to lay His head.* He also used to say, 'When the Lord remained in the desert, where He prayed and fasted forty days and forty nights, He did not have a cell or house built for Him there, but sheltered beneath the rocks in the mountains.' So, after His example, he would not have any house or cell that could be called his own, nor did he ever have one built. Indeed, if ever he chanced to say to the friars, 'Go and make that cell ready,' he would not afterwards live in it, because of that saying in the holy Gospel, *Be not anxious, etc.* For even at the time of his death he had it written in his Testament that all cells and houses of the friars were to be built only of wood and clay, the better to safeguard poverty and humility.

The Saint's purpose and method of choosing building sites in towns.

ONCE when blessed Francis was in Siena for treatment of his disease of the eyes, Master Bonaventura (*not the Saint*), who had given the friars the land on which the friary was built, said to him, 'Father, how do you like this place?' And blessed Francis said to him, 'Do you wish me to explain how the houses of the friars should be built?' 'Please do, Father,' he replied. And blessed Francis said, 'When the friars come to any city where they have no house, and meet anyone there who is willing to give them sufficient land to build a house, have a garden, and all that is necessary, they should first reckon how much land is sufficient for them, always bearing in mind holy poverty and the good example that we are obliged to show in all things.'

This he said because he did not want the friars to transgress against poverty in any way, either in their houses, churches, gardens, or anything else that they used. He did not wish them to possess places by right of ownership, but to live in them *as strangers and exiles*. This was why he did not wish the friars to live together in large numbers in their houses, because he thought it difficult to observe poverty in a large community. And from the beginning of his conversion until his death it was his intention that absolute poverty should be observed in all things.

'When the friars have examined the land necessary for a house,' he said, 'they should go to the Bishop of that city and say to him, "My Lord, so-and-so is willing to give us so much land for the love of God and for the salvation of his soul, so that we may build a house there. We are therefore coming to you first of all, because you are the father and lord of the souls of all the flock entrusted to you, as well as of ourselves and of all the brethren who will dwell in this place. So, with God's blessing and your own, we would like to build there." '

He spoke thus because the harvest of souls which the friars desire to gather is more readily obtained by working in harmony with the clergy, thereby helping both them and the people, than by antagonizing them, even though they may win the people. And he said, 'The Lord has called us to maintain His Faith, and support the Bishops and clergy of Holy Church. So we are bound always to love, honour and respect them to the best of our ability. For, as their name implies, the Friars are called Minors because they ought to be more humble than all other men in this world, both in example and in action. At the beginning of my conversion the Lord put His word into the mouth of the Bishop of Assisi so that he might counsel me rightly and strengthen me in the service of Christ; because of this and many other excellent virtues that I see in prelates, I wish to love and respect not only the Bishops but the poor priests as well, and to regard them as my masters.

'When the friars have received the blessing of the Bishop, let them go and mark out the boundaries of the land which they have accepted for their house, and as a sign of holy poverty and humility, let them plant a hedge instead of building a wall. Afterwards let them erect simple little huts of clay and wood, and a number of cells where the friars can pray or work from time to time in order to increase their merit and avoid idleness. Their churches are to be small; they are not to build great churches in order to preach to the people, or for any other reason, for they show greater humility and a better example when they visit other churches to preach. And should prelates or clergy, whether Religious or secular, visit their houses, their humble little dwellings, cells, and tiny churches will speak for themselves, and these things will edify them more than any words.'

He said also, 'Friars often raise large buildings, and violate our holy poverty, and by so doing provoke criticism and set a bad example. And sometimes, in order to obtain a better or holier place, or a larger congregation, they abandon their own houses out of covetousness and greed; or they pull them down and build others that are large and pretentious. Consequently those who have contributed to their cost, and others who see it, are greatly offended and distressed. So it is better for friars to erect humble little buildings, remaining loyal to their profession and setting a good example to their neighbours, rather than to act contrary to their profession and set a bad example to others. But should the friars ever leave a poor little house for one in a more suitable place, the offence caused would be less.'

11

How friars, especially those who had been prelates and scholars, opposed Saint Francis's desire to erect humble friaries and buildings.

As a sign of holy poverty, and humility blessed Francis decreed that the churches of the friars were to be small and their houses built only of wood and clay. For he wanted the friary of Saint Mary of the Porziuncula to be a pattern especially for buildings constructed of wood and clay, so that it might be a permanent memorial for all friars, present and to come, since it was the first and chief house of the whole Order. But some of the friars opposed him in this matter, saying that in some Provinces timber was more costly than stone, so that it did not seem sensible to them that their houses should be built of wood and clay.

But blessed Francis refused to argue with them, especially since he was nearing death and seriously ill. So he caused it to be written in his Testament: *Friars are to beware of accepting churches, houses, and all other places built for them unless they conform to holy poverty; and they are always to lodge in them as strangers and pilgrims.*

But we, who were with him when he wrote the Rule and most of his other writings, testify that he had many things written in the Rule and in his other writings to which many friars were opposed, especially the prelates and scholars among us; and to-day these things would have been very beneficial and valuable to the whole Order. But he had a great fear of scandal, and yielded, although with reluctance, to the wishes of the brethren. But he often said: 'Woe to those friars who oppose me in this matter, which I am firmly convinced to be the will of God for the greater usefulness and needs of the whole Order, although I unwillingly submit to their wish.' So he often used to say to his companions, 'It causes me great grief and distress that in these matters, which I learn from God with great effort in prayer and meditation, and which I know to be in accordance with His will, certain brethren who rely on their own experience and false prudence, oppose me and render them ineffective, saying, "These things are to be held and observed, and not those." '

12

How he regarded it as theft to obtain alms beyond one's needs.

BLESSED Francis used to say to his friars, 'I have never been a thief in the matter of alms, and obtained or used more than I needed. I have always accepted less than my needs, lest other poor folk should be cheated of their share; for to act otherwise would be theft.'

13

How Christ told blessed Francis that He did not wish friars to possess anything, either in common or individually.

WHEN the Friar Ministers urged him to allow the friars to possess something, at least, in common, so that so great a company might have some resources, blessed Francis called upon Christ in prayer, and took counsel with Him on the matter. And Christ at once answered him, saying, 'It is My will to withhold all things from them, both in general and in particular. I will always be ready to provide for this family, however great it may become, and I will always cherish it so long as it shall trust in Me.'

14

Saint Francis's hatred of money, and how he punished a friar who touched money.

FRANCIS, the true friend and imitator of Christ, utterly despised all things belonging to this world, and hated money above all else. He always urged his brethren both by word and example to avoid it as they would the devil. And he told the friars to have as little love and use for money as for dung.

One day, a layman happened to enter Saint Mary of the Porziuncula to pray, and laid some money near the cross as an offering. When he had left, one of the friars unthinkingly picked it up and placed it on a window ledge. But when this was reported to blessed Francis, this friar, realizing himself detected, at once hastened to ask forgiveness; and, falling to the ground, offered himself for punishment.

The holy Father reproved him, and took him severely to task for touching the money; and he ordered him to take the money from the window in his mouth, carry it outside the friary, and lay it on a heap of ass's dung.

When this friar readily obeyed this order, all who saw or heard were filled with the greatest fear, and thenceforward despised money as ass's dung. And further examples moved them to despise it altogether.

On avoiding luxury and many changes of clothing; and on being patient in privations.

BLESSED Francis, endowed with virtue from on high, was warmed by divine fire within rather than by outward clothing. He strongly disapproved of those in the Order who wore three garments and used finer clothing than necessary. He used to say that any need revealed by a love of pleasure and not by reason was the sign of a dead spirit, for 'when the spirit becomes lukewarm and inward grace grows cold, it follows that flesh and blood seek their own pleasures.' He also used to say, 'When the soul lacks any desire for spiritual joys, the flesh is bound to turn to its own. Then the lower desires plead the excuse of necessity, and the desires of the flesh influence the conscience. But if a genuine need besets any Brother and he immediately hastens to satisfy it, what reward can he expect? For an opportunity has arisen to win merit, but he has already shown clearly that he has no desire for it. For to refuse to endure these wants patiently is nothing but a return to Egypt' (*Exod.* xvi. 2).

Lastly, he desired that friars should on no account possess more than two habits, although he allowed these to be lined with patches stitched together. He used to say that choice materials were abhorrent, and sharply rebuked those who acted contrary to this; and in order to shame such people by his own example, he always repaired his own habit with rough sacking. For this reason, even in death he directed that his burial habit was to be covered with sacking. But if any friars were troubled by sickness, or had other needs, he would allow them another soft garment next the skin, provided that austerity and roughness was always maintained in their outer garment. For he used to say with the greatest sorrow, 'Henceforward strictness will be so greatly relaxed and lukewarmness rule, that the sons of a poor Father will not be ashamed to wear scarlet cloth, only the colour being changed.'

16

How he refused to comfort his own body with things that he thought other friars might lack.

WHILE blessed Francis was staying in the hermitage of Saint Eleutherius near Rieti, he lined his own habit and those of his companions with some pieces of cloth because of the intense cold—for, as was his custom, he had only one habit—and as a result his body began to derive a little comfort. A short while afterwards, when he returned from prayer, he said with great joy to his companion, 'It is my duty to be the pattern and example to all the brethren; so although it is necessary for my body to have a lined habit, I must consider my other brethren who have the same needs, and who perhaps do not and cannot possess it. I must therefore have sympathy with them in this matter, and endure the same privations as they, so that when they see me doing so, they may have the strength to bear theirs patiently.'

But we who were with him cannot express either in words or writing how many great necessities he denied his body in order to give a good example to the friars, and help them to bear their poverty patiently. For once the friars began to increase in numbers, he made it his chief and particular concern to teach the brethren what they should do or avoid by his own actions rather than by words.

17

How he was ashamed to see anyone poorer than himself.

ONCE, when he had met a poor man and considered his poverty, he said to his companion, 'This man's poverty brings great shame on us, and is a stern rebuke to our own. For since I have chosen holy poverty as my lady, my delight, and my spiritual and bodily treasure, I feel the greatest shame when I find someone poorer than myself. And the story has gone round the whole world that I am vowed to poverty before God and men.'

18

How, when the first friars were ashamed, he encouraged and taught them to go out and seek alms.

WHEN blessed Francis began to have friars he was full of joy at their conversion, and that God had given him a goodly company. And he had such love and respect for them that he did not insist that they went out for alms, because it was clear to him that they were ashamed to go. So, in order to spare them the shame, he used to go out every day to collect alms alone. But he had been accustomed to comfort in the world, was frail by nature, and was further weakened by overmuch fasting and hardship. And when he became exhausted by his efforts, he realized that he could not continue this work singlehanded. He knew, also, that his brethren were called to the same way of life, although they were ashamed to follow it; for as yet they did not fully realize this, nor were they discerning enough to say, 'We also will go out for alms.'

So he said to them, 'My dearest brothers, little children, do not be ashamed to go out for alms, for our Lord made Himself poor in this world for our sakes, and we have chosen to follow His example on the road of true poverty. This is our heritage, which our Lord Jesus Christ has won and bequeathed to us and to all who desire to live after His example in most holy poverty. I solemnly assure you that many of the noblest and wisest men of this age will join our company and regard it as a great honour to go out begging. So go out for alms confidently and gladly with the blessing of God. You should be more willing and happy to go for alms than a man who brings back an hundred coins in exchange for one, because you are offering the love of God to those from whom you ask alms when you say, "Give us alms for the love of the Lord God," for in comparison with Him heaven and earth are as nothing.'

But because the friars were as yet few in number, he could not send them out two by two, but he sent them singly through the towns and villages. So when they returned with the alms they had obtained, each of them showed blessed Francis the alms that he had received. And one would say to another, 'I have received more alms than you.' And blessed Francis was glad when he saw them so happy and cheerful. And thenceforward each of them readily asked permission to go out begging.

19

How he did not wish the friars to be provident and anxious for
to-morrow.

WHILE blessed Francis was with the first friars, he lived with them in such poverty that they observed the holy Gospel to the letter in all things and through all things, from the very day when our Lord revealed to him that he and his friars were to live according to the pattern of the holy Gospel. He therefore forbade the friar who cooked for the brethren to put dried beans into warm water in the evening, as is usual, when he intended to give them to the friars to eat on the following day. This was in order to observe the saying of the holy Gospel, *Do not fret over to-morrow*. So the friar delayed putting them to soften until after Matins on the day when they were to be eaten. Many friars, especially in towns, continued to observe this custom for a long time, and would not seek or accept more alms than were necessary to support them for a single day.

How by word and example he reproved friars who had prepared a lavish meal on Christmas Day because a Minister was present.

WHEN one of the Friar-Ministers had visited blessed Francis in order to keep the Feast of Christmas with him in the friary at Rieti, the friars prepared the tables rather elaborately and carefully on Christmas Day in honour of the Minister, putting on fair white linen and glass vessels. But when the Father came down from his cell to eat, and saw the tables raised up from the ground and prepared with such great care, he went back secretly and took the hat and staff of a poor beggar who had arrived that day. And calling in a low voice to one of his companions, he went out of the door of the friary unseen by the brethren in the house, while his companion remained inside near the door. Meanwhile the friars came in to dine, for blessed Francis had ordered that, whenever he did not come at once at mealtime, the friars were not to wait for him.

When he had stood outside for a while, he knocked on the door, and his companion immediately opened to him. And entering with his hat on his back and his staff in his hand, he came like a stranger or beggar to the door of the room where the friars were eating, and called out, 'For the love of God, give alms to this poor sick stranger!' But the Minister and the other friars recognized him at once. And the Minister replied, 'Brother, we are poor as well, and because we are so many, the alms that we have only meet our needs. But for the love of God which you have invoked, come in and we will share with you the alms which the Lord has given us.'

When he had entered and stood before the friars' table, the Minister handed to him the plate from which he was eating, and also some bread. And taking it, he humbly sat down on the floor beside the fire in the sight of the friars sitting at table. Then he sighed and said to the brethren, 'When I saw the table elaborately and carefully laid, I felt that this was not the table of poor religious who go around for alms from door to door each day. Dearest brothers, we are under a greater obligation than other Religious to follow the example of Christ's humility and poverty, for it is to this end that we have been called and professed before God and men. So it seems to me that I am sitting like a Friar Minor, because the feasts of our Lord and the Saints are better honoured in the want and poverty by which these Saints won heaven than in the luxury and excess by which a soul is estranged from heaven.'

The friars were ashamed at his words, realizing that he was speaking no more than the truth. And seeing him seated on the ground, wishing to correct and teach them in such a holy and simple way, some of them began to weep aloud. For he warned the brethren to eat humbly and simply, so as to edify lay folk. And if any poor man should visit them or be invited by the friars, he was to sit with them as an equal, and not the poor man on the floor and the friars on high.

21

How the Lord Bishop of Ostia wept and was edified by the poverty of the friars at the time of the Chapter.

WHEN the Lord Bishop of Ostia, who later became Pope Gregory (IX), attended the Chapter of the friars at Saint Mary of the Porziuncula, he entered the house with many knights and clergy to see the friars' dormitory. And seeing how the friars lay on the ground and had nothing beneath them but a little straw, and a few poor broken-down pallets, and no pillows, he began to weep freely before them all, saying, 'Look how the friars sleep here! But we, wretched creatures, enjoy so many luxuries! What will become of us?' So he and all the others were much edified. He did not even find a table in the place, because the friars used to eat on the ground; for as long as blessed Francis lived, all the friars in that house used to eat on the ground.

22

How, at blessed Francis's advice, the soldiers obtained their needs by asking alms from door to door.

WHEN blessed Francis was in the friary at Bagni near the city of Nocera, his feet began to swell badly because of the disease of dropsy, and he became seriously ill. When the people of Assisi heard of this, they hurriedly sent soldiers to the friary to escort him to Assisi, fearing that if he remained there, others would obtain his most holy body. But while they were bringing him, they stopped in a fortress-town belonging to the Commune of Assisi in order to eat; and blessed Francis rested in the house of a poor man who welcomed him willingly and gladly. Meanwhile the soldiers went through the town to buy themselves what they needed, and found nothing. So they came back to the holy Father and told him jokingly, 'Brother, you will have to let us share your alms, for we cannot buy anything to eat!' Then blessed Francis said to them with great fervour, 'You have not found anything because you trusted in your flies (*meaning, your money*), and not in God. Go back to the houses where you went trying to buy food; put aside your shame, and ask alms for the love of the Lord God. The Holy Spirit will move them to give generously.' So they went away and asked alms as blessed Francis had told them; and those from whom they asked alms gave them whatever they had with great gladness and generosity. And recognizing that a miracle had happened to them, they returned to blessed Francis praising God with great joy.

The holy Father used to regard it as an act of great nobility and dignity before God and the world to ask alms for love of the Lord God, for all things which our heavenly Father has created

35

for the use of men are granted freely despite their sin both to the worthy and to the unworthy through the love of His beloved Son. He used to say that the servant of God ought to ask alms for the love of God more willingly and gladly than one who, out of his own generosity and sympathy, might go and say, 'If anyone will give me a penny, I will give him a thousand pieces of gold.' For, by asking alms, the servant of God offers the love of God to those of whom he begs, and in comparison with this all things in heaven and earth are nothing.

So before the friars increased in numbers, and even after they became numerous, whenever a friar went through the world preaching, and was invited by anyone, however noble or wealthy, to eat and lodge with him, he would always go for alms at meal-time before he came to his host's house, in order to uphold the good example of the friars and the dignity of Lady Poverty. Blessed Francis often used to say to his host, 'I will not resign my royal dignity and heritage, and my profession and that of my brethren (that is, to beg bread from door to door).' And sometimes his host would go with him and carry the alms which blessed Francis had collected, and preserve them like relics out of devotion to him.

The writer has seen this happen many times, and testifies to these things.

23

How he went out for alms before he would go in to the Cardinal's table.

ONCE when blessed Francis was visiting the Lord Bishop of Ostia, who later became Pope Gregory (IX), he went out un-observed at dinner-time in order to ask alms from door to door. And when he returned, the Lord of Ostia had already gone in to table with many knights and nobles. But when the holy Father entered, he laid the alms that he had collected on the table before the Cardinal, and sat down beside him, for the Cardinal always wished that blessed Francis should sit next him at table. The Cardinal was somewhat embarrassed to find that blessed Francis had gone out for alms and laid them on the table; but he said nothing at the time because of his guests.

When blessed Francis had eaten a little, he took up his alms and in the name of the Lord God distributed a little to each of the knights and chaplains of the Lord Cardinal. And they all accepted them with great reverence and devotion, reaching out their hoods and sleeves; and some ate the alms, while others kept them out of devotion to him.

After dinner the Cardinal entered his own apartment, taking blessed Francis with him. And stretching out his arms, he embraced him with great joy and gladness, saying, 'My simple brother, why have you shamed me to-day by going out for alms when you visit my house, which is a home for your friars?' 'On the contrary, my lord,' replied blessed Francis, 'I have shown you the greatest honour; for when a servant does his duty and fulfils his obedience to his lord, he does honour to his lord.' And he said, 'It is my duty to be the pattern and example of our poor friars, especially as I know that in this Order of friars there are, and will be, friars who are Minors in name and in deed, who, for love of the Lord God and by the anointing of the Holy Spirit Who will guide them in all things, will be humble and obedient, and the servants of their brethren. There are also, and will be, some among them who are held back by shame or bad custom, and who scorn to humble themselves and stoop to going for alms and doing other servile work. Because of this I must by my own actions teach those who belong, and will belong, to the Order, that they are inexcusable in the eyes of God both in this life and in the life to come. So while I am with you, who are our Lord and Apostolic Protector, or with other great and wealthy men of this world who for love of God not only receive me into your houses but even press me to eat at your table, I will not be ashamed to go out for alms.

Indeed, I intend to regard and retain this practice as the highest nobility and royal dignity, and to do it in honour of Him Who, though He was Lord of all, willed for our sakes to become the servant of all. And when He was rich and glorious in His majesty, He came as one poor and despised in our humility. So I want all present or future friars to know that I regard it as a greater consolation of soul and body to sit at the poor little table of the brethren, and to see in front of me the meagre alms that they beg from door to door for love of the Lord God, than to sit at your table and that of other lords, abundantly provided with different dishes. For the bread of charity is holy bread, hallowed by the praise and love of God, and when a friar goes out for alms he should first say, "Praised and blessed be the Lord God!" And afterwards he should say, "Give us alms for love of the Lord God." '

The Cardinal was much edified by the holy Father's words, and said, 'My son, do whatever seems good to you, for God is with you, and you with Him.' For, as blessed Francis often said, it was his wish that no friar should remain long without going out to beg alms, both because of its great merit, and lest he should become ashamed to go. Indeed, the nobler and greater a friar had been in the world, the more pleased and edified he was when he went for alms and did other humble work as the friars were then accustomed to do.

24

On the friar who neither prayed nor worked, but ate well.

IN the early days of the Order, when the friars were living at Rivo Torto near Assisi, there was one friar among them who prayed little and did no work; he refused to go out for alms, but used to eat heartily. Thinking the matter over, blessed Francis knew by the Holy Spirit that the man was a lover of the flesh,

and said to him, 'Be off with you, Brother Fly, since you want
to eat up the labours of your brethren, and be idle in the work of
God. You are like a barren and idle drone, who gathers nothing
and does no work, but consumes the toil and gain of the good
bees!'

So he went his way, and because he was a lover of the flesh,
he neither asked mercy nor found it.

25

*How he went out with fervour to meet a beggar who was walking along
with his alms and praising God.*

ON another occasion, when blessed Francis was at S. Mary of
the Porziuncula, a friar of true spiritual poverty was coming
along the street on his way back from Assisi with alms, and as he
walked he was cheerfully singing God's praises in a loud voice.
As he drew near the church of S. Mary, blessed Francis heard
him, and at once went out to meet him with the greatest fervour
and joy. He ran up to him in the road, and joyfully kissed the
shoulder on which he was carrying a bag with alms. Then he
took the bag from his shoulder, laid it on his own shoulder,
and thus bore it into the friary. And he told the brethren, 'This
is how I want a friar of mine to go out and return with alms,
happy, joyful, and praising God.'

26

*How the Lord revealed to him that the friars were to be called Minors,
and were to proclaim peace and salvation.*

ONE day blessed Francis said, 'The Order and life of the Friars
Minor is a little flock which the Son of God has asked of His
heavenly Father in these latter days, saying, "Father, I would that

Thou shouldest form and give Me a new and humble people in these latter days, who will be unlike all others who have preceded them in humility and poverty, and content to possess Me alone." And the Father said to His beloved Son, "My Son, it is done as Thou hast asked." '

So blessed Francis used to say that God willed and revealed to him that they should be called Friars Minor, because they were to be the poor and humble people whom the Son of God had asked of His Father. Of this people the Son of God Himself speaks in the Gospel: *Do not be afraid, My little flock. Your Father has determined to give you His kingdom.* And again: *Believe Me, when you did it to one of the least of My brethren here, you did it to Me.* And although the Lord was speaking of all poor and spiritual people, He was referring more particularly to the Order of Friars Minor which was to arise in His Church.

Therefore, since it was revealed to blessed Francis that it should be called the Order of Friars Minor, he caused it to be written in his first Rule, which he took before the Lord Pope Innocent III; who approved and granted it, and later proclaimed it publicly in Consistory.

The Lord also revealed to him the greeting which the friars were to use, and he caused this to be written in his Testament, saying: *The Lord revealed to me that I should say as a greeting, 'The Lord give you peace.'*

In the early days of the Order, while he was travelling with a friar who was one of the first twelve, he used to greet men and women along the road and in the fields, saying, 'The Lord give you peace.' And because people had never heard such a greeting from any Religious, they were very startled. Indeed, some said indignantly, 'What do you mean by this greeting of yours?' As a result the friar became embarrassed, and said to blessed Francis, 'Allow me to use some other greeting.' But the holy Father said, 'Let them chatter, for they do not understand the ways of God. Don't feel ashamed because of this, for one day the nobles and princes of this world will respect you and the other friars for this greeting. For it is no marvel if the Lord should desire to have a new little flock, whose speech and way of life are unlike those of all its predecessors, and which is content to possess Him alone, the Most High and most glorious.'

Part II

ON CHARITY AND COMPASSION TOWARDS ONE'S NEIGHBOUR

27

Firstly, how blessed Francis made concessions to a friar who was dying of hunger by eating with him, and how he warned the friars to use discretion in their penance.

DURING the period when blessed Francis began to have brethren, and was living with them at Rivo Torto near Assisi, one night while all the brethren were asleep one of the friars cried out, saying, 'I am dying! I am dying!' Startled and frightened, all the friars awoke. Blessed Francis got up and said, 'Rise, brothers, and light a lamp.' And when it was lit, he said, 'Who was it who said, "I am dying"?' The friar answered, 'It is I.' And he said, 'What is the matter, brother? How are you dying?' And he said, 'I am dying of hunger.'

The holy Father at once ordered food to be brought, and having great charity and discretion, he ate with him lest he should be ashamed to eat alone; and, at his wish, all the other friars joined them. For that friar and all the others were newly converted to the Lord, and used to discipline their bodies without restraint. After they had eaten blessed Francis said to the other friars, 'My brothers, everyone must consider his own constitution, for although one of you may be able to sustain his body on less food, I do not want another who needs more food to try and imitate him in this matter. Each brother must consider his own constitution and allow his body its needs, so that it has the strength to serve the spirit. For while we are bound to avoid over-indulgence in food, which injures both body and soul, we must also avoid excessive abstinence, especially as the Lord *desires mercy, and not sacrifice*.' And he added, 'Dearest brothers, necessity and charity for my brother have moved me to act as I have done, and we have eaten with him lest he be ashamed to eat alone. But I do not wish to do so again, for it would be neither regular nor fitting. It is my wish and command that each of you is to satisfy his body as need demands and so far as our poverty allows.'

For the first friars, and those who followed them for a long while, afflicted their bodies beyond measure by abstinence from food and drink, by vigils, by cold, by coarse clothing, and by manual labour. They wore iron bands and breast-plates, and the roughest of hair shirts. So the holy Father, considering that the friars might fall ill as a result of this—as had already happened in a short time—gave orders in Chapter that no friar should wear anything but the habit next his skin.

But we who were with him bear witness that although he was discreet and moderate towards the brethren throughout his life, this was in order that they should never fall away from poverty and the spirit of our Order. Nevertheless, from the beginning of his conversion until the end of his life, the most holy Father was severe towards his own body, although he was frail by nature and while in the world could not have lived without comfort. At one time, therefore, considering that the friars were exceeding the bounds of poverty and sincerity in food and other matters, he said to a number of friars as representing all the brethren, 'Do not let the brethren imagine that any concession is necessary to my own body. For since it is my duty to be a pattern and example to all the friars, I wish to have, and to be content with, scanty and very poor food, and to make use of all other things in the spirit of poverty, and to shun delicate food altogether.'

How he made a concession to a sick friar by eating grapes with him.

ON another occasion, while blessed Francis was living in the same place, one of the friars, who was a spiritual man and an early member of the Order, was ill and very weak. As he looked at him, the holy Father felt great compassion for him. But because at that time the friars, both healthy and sick, were cheerfully regarding their poverty as plenty, and would not use or ask for medicines in sickness, but willingly accepted bodily privations, blessed Francis said to himself, 'If only this brother could eat some ripe grapes first thing in the morning, I think they would do him good.'

And he acted on this idea, for he rose very early one day, and calling the friar to him privately, led him into a vineyard near the friary. Choosing a vine where the grapes were good to eat, he sat down beside the vine with the friar, and began to eat the grapes lest the brother should be ashamed to eat alone. And as they ate the friar was cured, and they praised God together. This friar remembered the compassion and kindness of the most holy Father for the rest of his life, and often used to tell the brethren about it with devotion and tears.

29

How he stripped himself and his companion to provide clothing for a poor old woman.

AT Celano, one winter, blessed Francis had a length of cloth folded to form a cloak, which a friend of the friars had lent him. When an old woman came to him asking alms, he immediately took the cloth from his shoulders, and although it did not belong to him, he gave it to the poor old woman, saying, 'Go and make a garment for yourself, for you need it badly enough!'

The old woman laughed and was astonished—whether from fear or joy I cannot say—and took the cloth from his hands. Fearing that if she delayed he might take it back, she hurried away and cut up the cloth with shears. But when she discovered that the cloth was not sufficient for a garment, she put her trust in the kindness already shown by the holy Father, and told him that the cloth was not sufficient for a garment.

The Saint looked at his companion, who was wearing a similar piece of cloth on his shoulders, and said, 'Do you hear what this poor woman says? Let us put up with the cold for the love of God, and give the cloth to this poor woman so that her garment can be completed.' And at once his companion gave her his own, just as blessed Francis had done. So both of them remained without a cloak in order that the poor woman might be clothed.

30

How he regarded it as robbery not to give a cloak to one who had greater need.

ONCE when he was returning from Siena, he met a poor man on the road, and said to his companion, 'We ought to return this cloak to the poor man, whose it is; for we have accepted it as a loan until we should find someone poorer than ourselves.' But knowing how badly the generous Father needed it, his companion protested strongly that he should not neglect himself to provide for someone else. But the Saint said to him, 'I refuse to be a thief, for we should be guilty of theft if we refused to give it to one more poor than ourselves.' So the kindly Father gave away the cloak to the poor man.

How he gave a cloak to a poor man on a certain condition.

AT Celle di Cortona blessed Francis was wearing a new cloak which the friars had taken great trouble to obtain for him. But when a poor man came to the friary, weeping for his dead wife and poverty-stricken, bereaved family, the compassionate Saint said to him, 'I give you this cloak on condition that you part with it to no one unless he buys it from you and pays a good price.' Hearing this, the friars ran to take the cloak away from the poor man; but taking courage from the face of the holy Father, he clung to it with both hands. And at length the friars bought back the cloak, and paid a fair price for it to the poor man.

32

How, through the alms of blessed Francis, a poor man forgave his injuries and abandoned his hatred for his master.

AT Celle, in the lordship of Perugia, blessed Francis met a poor man whom he had formerly known in the world, and asked him, 'Brother, how are things with you?' But the man began to utter angry curses on his master, saying, 'Thanks to my master—God curse him!—I have had nothing but misfortune, for he has stripped me of all that I possess.'

Seeing him persist in mortal hatred, blessed Francis was filled with pity for his soul, and said, 'Brother, pardon your master for the love of God, and free your own soul; it is possible that he will restore to you whatever he has taken away. Otherwise, you have lost your goods and will lose your soul as well.' And the man said, 'I cannot fully forgive him unless he first restores to me what he has taken away.' Then blessed Francis said to him, 'Look, I will give you this cloak; I beg you to forgive your master for the love of the Lord God.' And at once his heart was melted and touched by this act of kindness, and he forgave his master his wrongs.

33

How he sent a cloak to a poor woman who, like himself, suffered from her eyes.

A POOR woman of Machilone came to Rieti to be treated for a disease of the eyes. And when the doctor visited blessed Francis, he said to him, 'Brother, a woman has come to me with a disease of the eyes, and she is so poor that I have to pay her expenses myself.' As soon as he heard this he was moved with pity for her, and calling one of the friars who was his Guardian, he said to him, 'Brother Guardian, we have to repay a loan.' 'What is this loan?' asked the Guardian. And he said, 'This cloak, which we have borrowed from a poor, sick woman, and which we must return to her.' And the Guardian said, 'Do whatever seems best to you, Brother.'

Then blessed Francis, with great merriment, called a friend of his who was a spiritual man, and told him, 'Take this cloak, and twelve loaves with it, and go to this poor woman with a disease of the eyes whom the doctor will point out to you. And say to her, "The poor man to whom you lent this cloak thanks you for the loan of it; take back what belongs to you." ' So he went and said to the woman all that blessed Francis had told him. But thinking that he was making a fool of her, she was nervous and embarrassed, saying, 'Leave me in peace; I don't know what you are talking about.' But he laid the cloak and the twelve loaves in her hands. Then, realizing that he was speaking in earnest, she accepted them with fear and reverence, rejoicing and praising the Lord. And afraid that they might be taken from her, she rose secretly by night and returned home with joy. But blessed Francis had arranged with the Guardian to pay her expenses daily as long as she remained there.

We who lived with him testify to the greatness of his charity and compassion towards sick and healthy alike, both to his own friars and to other poor folk. For after persuading us not to be upset, he used to give away to the poor with great inward and outward joy even his own bodily necessities, which the friars had sometimes obtained with great trouble and difficulty, thus depriving himself even of things that he badly needed. Because of this the Minister General and his Guardian told him not to give away his habit to any friar without their permission. For in their devotion to him the friars used sometimes to ask him for his habit, and at once he would give it; but sometimes he divided it and gave away a portion, retaining part for himself, for he wore only a single habit.

34

How he gave away his habit to friars who asked it for the love of God.

WHEN he was travelling through one of the Provinces preaching, two French friars met him. And having received great consolation from him, they finally begged his habit for the love of God. And as soon as he heard 'for the love of God,' he took off his habit and gave it to them, remaining unclothed for a good while. For when anyone invoked the love of God he would never refuse his cord, or habit, or anything that they asked. But he was very displeased, and often rebuked the friars, when he heard them use the words 'for the love of God' without good cause. For he used to say, 'The love of God is so sublime and precious that it should only be mentioned on rare occasions and in great need, and then with great reverence.'

But one of these friars removed his own habit, and gave it to him in exchange. Whenever he gave away his own habit, or part of it to anyone, he suffered great want and distress, because he could not obtain another or have it made quickly, especially as he always wished to have a shabby habit, patched up with pieces of cloth, sometimes both inside and out. Indeed, he would seldom or never wear a new habit, but obtained an old habit from another friar. And sometimes he would obtain part of his habit from one friar, and part from another. But at times he used to line it inside with new cloth, because of his frequent illnesses and chills of the stomach and spleen. He observed this absolute poverty in clothing up to the very year in which he departed to the Lord. For, a few days before his death, since he was suffering from dropsy and almost dried up by his many ailments, the friars made him several habits, so that his habit could be changed night or day whenever necessary.

35

How he wished to give some cloth to a poor man secretly.

ON another occasion a poor man came to the friary where blessed Francis was staying, and begged a piece of cloth from the friars for the love of God. When he heard of this, the holy Father said to one of the friars, 'Search through the house, and see if you can find any length or piece of cloth, and give it to this poor man.' But having gone around the whole house, the friar told him that he could find nothing.

So in order that the poor man should not go away empty-handed, blessed Francis stole away quietly—lest the Guardian should forbid him—and took a knife. Then he sat down in a remote place and began to cut away part of his habit which was sewed on the inside, intending to give it to the poor man secretly. But the Guardian noticed him, and at once forbade him to give it away, especially as there was a hard frost at the time, and he was very frail and cold. So the holy Father said to him, 'If you do not want me to give the man this piece, you must make sure that some other piece is given to our poor brother.' And at the insistence of blessed Francis, the friars gave the poor man some cloth from their own garments.

Whenever he travelled about the world preaching, if any brother lent him a cloak, he would not accept it unless he was allowed to give it to any poor man whom he met or who came to him, if the voice of his own conscience told him that it was necessary to that person. He always went on foot, and only rode a donkey after he became ill. Only in the most pressing need would he use a horse; normally he refused to ride at all, and only did so a short while before his death.

36

How he told Brother Giles, before he was received into the Order, to give his cloak to a poor man.

AT the beginning of the Order, when he was living at Rivo Torto with only two friars, a man named Giles, who became the third friar, came to him from the world in order to share his way of life. And when he had remained there for some days, still wearing his secular clothes, a poor man came to the place asking alms of blessed Francis. Turning to Giles, blessed Francis said to him, 'Give this poor brother your cloak.' At once Giles gladly removed it from his back and gave it to the poor man. Then it became clear to him that God had imparted a new grace to his heart, since he had given his cloak to the poor man with great cheerfulness. So he was received into the Order by blessed Francis, and constantly advanced in virtue to the greatest perfection.

37

On the penance that he imposed on a friar who had wrongfully criticized a certain poor man.

WHEN blessed Francis had gone to preach at a house of the friars near Rocca Brizzi, it happened that on the day he was due to preach, a poor, sick man came to him. Full of compassion for him, he began to speak about the man's poverty and sickness to his companion. And his companion said to him, 'Brother, it is true that this man seems poor enough, but it may be that no one in the whole Province has a greater desire for riches.' He was at once severely rebuked by blessed Francis, and confessed his fault. Then the Father said to him, 'Are you ready to perform the penance that I give you?' 'I will do it willingly,' he replied. And he said to him, 'Go and remove your habit, and throw yourself naked at the poor man's feet, and tell him how you have sinned in speaking ill of him, and ask him to pray for you.' So the friar went and did all that blessed Francis had told him. Then he rose and resumed his habit, and returned to blessed Francis. And the Father said to him, 'Do you want to know how you sinned against him, and against Christ Himself? Whenever you see a poor man, remember Christ in Whose Name he comes, and how He took upon Himself our poverty and weakness. For this man's poverty serves us as a mirror, in which we should view and consider with pity the weakness and poverty of our Lord Jesus Christ, which He endured in His own body for our salvation.'

38

How he ordered a New Testament to be given to a poor woman,
the mother of two friars.

ANOTHER time, while he was staying at S. Mary of the Porzi-uncula, a poor old woman, who had two sons in the Order, came to the friary asking alms of blessed Francis. He immediately asked Brother Peter Catanii, who was then Minister General, 'Have we anything to give our mother?' For he used to say that the mother of any friar was mother to himself and to all the friars. Brother Peter said to him, 'There is nothing in the house that we can give her, for she wants the kind of alms that can sustain her bodily needs. But in the church we have a single New Testament, from which we read the lessons at Matins.' (For at that time the friars had no breviaries and few psalters.) So blessed Francis said to him, 'Give the New Testament to our mother, so that she can sell it for her needs. I am sure that this will please our Lord and the Blessed Virgin better than if we were to read from it.' So he gave it to her. For it can be said and written of him as is read of blessed Job: *Loving care has borne me company as I grew up from childhood, ever since I left my mother's womb.*

To us who lived with him it would be a long and very difficult task to write or describe not only what we have learned from others about his charity and kindness toward the friars and other poor folk, but what we have seen with our own eyes.

PART III

ON THE PERFECTION OF HOLY HUMILITY AND OBEDIENCE IN BLESSED FRANCIS AND HIS FRIARS

39

Firstly, how he resigned his office as head of the Order, and appointed Friar Peter Catanii as Minister General.

IN order to preserve the virtue of holy humility, blessed Francis resigned the chief office before all the friars during a Chapter held a few years after his conversion, saying, 'I am now as though dead to you. Look to Peter Catanii, whom you and I will all obey.' And falling to his knees before him, he promised him obedience and reverence.

At this all the friars wept, and intolerable grief wrung deep groans from them when they saw themselves deprived of so great a Father in this way. But with eyes raised to heaven and hands clasped, the blessed Father rose and said, 'Lord, I commend to Thee the family which hitherto Thou hast entrusted to me. Because of my infirmities which Thou knowest, sweetest Lord, I now entrust it to the Ministers, for I no longer have the strength to care for it. They shall render account to Thee in the Day of Judgement, O Lord, if any friar shall have perished through their negligence, bad example, or harsh correction.'

Thenceforward until his death he remained subject to them, behaving himself more humbly in all things than any others.

How he gave up his own companion, not desiring to have any particular companion.

ON another occasion he gave up all his companions to his Vicar, saying, 'I do not wish to appear alone in the privilege of having an especial companion of my own. Let the friars accompany me from place to place as the Lord shall move them.' And he added, 'Recently I saw a blind man who had only a little dog to guide him on his way, and I do not want to seem better than he.'

For it was always his glory to renounce every trace of privilege and ostentation so that the virtue of Christ might dwell in him.

How the disloyalty of the Ministers caused him to surrender his office.

ONCE, when asked by one of the friars why he had abandoned his charge of the friars and entrusted them into the hands of others as though they did not belong to him at all, he replied, 'My son, I love the brethren to the utmost of my power, but if they would follow in my footsteps I should love them still more, and would not make myself a stranger to them. For some of the superiors pull them in another direction, holding up to them as patterns the men of long ago, and disregarding my warnings. But what they are doing and the way in which they are now acting will appear more clearly in the end.'

And shortly afterwards, when he was burdened with severe illness, he raised himself in bed, and cried out in vehemence of spirit, 'Who are these who have torn my Order and my friars out of my hands? If I come to the General Chapter I will make my intention clear!'

*How he humbly obtained meat for the sick, and urged them to be
humble and patient.*

BLESSED Francis was not ashamed to obtain meat for a sick friar
in the public places of cities, but he warned those who were ill
to endure want patiently, and not to create a disturbance when
there was not sufficient food for their needs.

So in the first Rule he caused this to be written: *I beg my sick
friars not to grow impatient in their infirmities, nor to complain against
the Lord or the brethren, nor to insist on having medicines, nor to have
an undue desire to liberate this swiftly-perishing body, which is the
enemy of the soul. But let them give thanks for all things, that they
may desire to be men such as God wills them to be; for those whom
the Lord has predestined to eternal life He trains with the spur of
scourges and infirmities. As He Himself says*: '*It is those I love that
I correct and chasten.*'

*The humble reply of blessed Francis and blessed Dominic when they
were both asked whether they were willing for their friars to become
prelates in the Church.*

IN the city of Rome, when those two illustrious lights of the
world, blessed Francis and blessed Dominic, were together in
the presence of the Lord Cardinal of Ostia, who later became
Pope, and when each in turn had spoken sweetly of God, my
Lord of Ostia at length said, 'In the primitive Church the
pastors and prelates were poor men, burning with charity, not
with greed. Why should we not choose bishops and prelates
from among your friars, so that they may influence all the others
by their witness and example?'

Then there arose a humble and devout dispute between the

Saints as to which of them was to reply, for neither wished to take precedence, but each deferred to the other, urging him to answer. But at length the humility of Francis prevailed, in that he did not answer first, while Dominic also prevailed, in that by answering first he also humbly obeyed.

So blessed Dominic said, 'My Lord, my friars have already been raised to a noble state if they will only realize it; and in so far as I am able, I will never permit them to obtain any shadow of dignity.' Then blessed Francis, bowing low before the Lord Cardinal, said, 'My Lord, my friars are called Minors so that they may not presume to become greater. Their vocation teaches them to remain in a humble place, and to follow in the footsteps of Christ's humility, so that by this means they may at last be exalted above others in the eyes of the Saints. So if you wish them to bear fruit in the Church of God, hold them to the observance of their vocation. And should they aspire to high place, thrust them down to their proper level, and never allow them to rise to any prelacy.'

Such were the replies of the Saints, and when they had ended, the Lord of Ostia was much edified by the answers of both, and gave profound thanks to God.

As they were both taking leave together, blessed Dominic asked blessed Francis if he would consent to give him the cord which he wore; but although he asked this favour out of love, blessed Francis refused it out of humility. At length Dominic's loving persistence prevailed, and having obtained the cord, he girded it beneath his habit and wore it devoutly from that time on.

Then each placed his hands between the hands of the other and commended himself to him with the most affectionate regard. And blessed Dominic said to blessed Francis, 'Brother Francis, I wish that your Order and mine could become one, and that we could live within the Church under the same Rule.' When at length they had taken leave of one another, blessed Dominic said to those standing by, 'I tell you in all truth that every Religious should imitate this holy man Francis, so great is the perfection of his sanctity.'

44

How, in order to establish humility, he wished all the friars to serve lepers.

FROM the first days of his conversion blessed Francis, like a wise builder, established himself with God's help on the firm rock of the perfect humility and poverty of the Son of God. And because of his own profound humility, he called his Order that of Friars Minor.

So at the commencement of the Order he wished the friars to live in leper-houses to serve them, and by so doing to establish themselves in holy humility. For whenever anyone, whether noble or commoner, entered the Order, among the other instructions given him, he was told that he must humbly serve the lepers and live with them in their houses, as was laid down in the Rule: *Seeking to possess nothing under heaven save holy poverty, in which they will be nourished by the Lord with food for body and soul in this world, and in the life to come will attain the heritage of heaven.*

So he laid foundations both for himself and others on the deepest poverty and humility, for when he might have become a great prelate in the Church of God, he chose and willed to be humble, not only in the Church but among his own friars as well. For in his opinion and desire, this lowliness was to be his highest dignity in the sight of God and men.

45

How he wished the glory and honour of all his good words and deeds to be given to God alone.

WHEN he had been preaching to the people of Terni in the town square, as soon as his sermon had ended, the bishop of the place, who was a discerning and spiritual man, rose and said to the people, 'From the beginning, when our Lord planted and founded His Church, He has always enlightened it through holy men who have fostered it by word and example. But now in these latter days He has enlightened it through this poor, undistinguished and unlearned man Francis. Therefore love and honour our Lord, and beware of sin; *for He has not dealt so with any other nation.*'

When he had ended speaking, the Bishop came down from the place where he had preached and entered the Cathedral. And blessed Francis went up to him, bowed before him, and threw himself at his feet, saying, 'My Lord Bishop, I assure you that no man in this world has ever done me such honour as you have done me this day. For other men say, "This is a holy man," and attribute glory and holiness to me, rather than the Creator. But you are a discerning man, and have distinguished between the precious and the worthless.'

For when blessed Francis was praised and called a saint, he used to answer such comments by saying: 'I am not as yet so secure that I might not have sons and daughters! For if at any time the Lord were to deprive me of the treasure that He has entrusted to me, what would remain to me but a body and a soul, and even unbelievers have this? In fact, I am quite sure that if the Lord had granted a thief or an unbeliever as many great gifts as He has to me, they would have been more faithful to Him than I. For in a picture of our Lord and the Blessed Virgin painted on wood, it is the Lord and the Blessed Virgin who receive honour, while the wood and the painting claim nothing for themselves; in the same way a servant of God is a kind of picture of God, in whom God is honoured for His favour. But he may not claim any credit for himself, for in comparison with God he is less than the wood and the painting; indeed, he is nothing at all. Honour and glory are to be given to God alone; but to a man himself nothing but shame and sorrow as long as he lives amid the miseries of this world.'

How until his death he wished to have one of his companions as his
Guardian, and to live under obedience.

WISHING to remain in perfect humility and obedience until
death, he said to the Minister General a long while before this,
'I would like you to transfer your own authority over me to
one of my companions, whom I will obey in your place; for
holy obedience is of such merit that I wish it to remain with me
both in life and death.' And thenceforward until his death
he had one of his own companions as his Guardian, and obeyed
him in the place of the Minister General. He once said to his
companions, 'The Lord has granted me this favour among
others, that if a novice who had entered the Order this very
day were assigned to me as Guardian, I would obey him as
gladly as one who is senior and of long standing in the Order.
For a man under authority should regard his superior not as a
man, but as God, for love of Whom he is subject to him.'
Later he said, 'Did I so wish it, the Lord could make me more
feared by my friars than any other Superior in the world. But
the Lord has granted me the favour of desiring to be content
with everything, as one who is of no account in the Order.'

As he himself testifies, we who lived with him have seen
with our own eyes how, when some of the friars did not provide
for his needs, or spoke to him in a way that usually provokes a
man, he at once went away to pray; and when he returned, he
would not recall anything, nor did he ever say, 'So-and-so
did not please me,' or, 'So-and-so said this to me.'

Persevering in this way of life, the nearer he drew to death,
the more careful he was to consider how he could live and die
in all humility and poverty, and in the perfecting of all virtues.

On the perfect way of obedience which he taught.

THE most holy Father used to say to his friars, 'Dearest brothers, carry out an order at once, and don't wait for it to be repeated. Don't plead or object that anything in a command is impossible, for if I were to order you to do something beyond your strength, holy obedience would not fail to support you.'

48

How he compared perfect obedience to a dead body.

ONCE, while he was sitting with his companions, he voiced this complaint: 'There is hardly a single Religious in the whole world who obeys his superior well!' His companions at once said to him, 'Tell us, Father, what is the perfect and best form of obedience?' In reply he described true and perfect obedience under the simile of a dead body. 'Take up a dead body,' he said, 'and lay it where you will. You will see that it does not resist being removed, or complain of its position, or ask to be left alone. If it is lifted on to a chair, it does not look up, but down. If it is clothed in purple, it looks paler than ever. In the same way, one who is truly obedient does not question why he is moved, does not mind where he is placed, and does not demand to be transferred. If he is promoted to high office, he remains as humble as before, and the more he is honoured, the more unworthy he considers himself.'

Whenever blessed Francis received direct and simple commands, rather than requests, he regarded them as commands under holy obedience. But he believed that the highest form of obedience, in which flesh and blood plays no part, is to go among the unbelievers under the inspiration of God, either to help one's fellow men or with a desire for martyrdom. He considered that to seek martyrdom was truly acceptable to God.

49

How it is dangerous to give an order under obedience too hastily, or to disobey an order given under obedience.

THE blessed Father considered that an order under obedience should be given but seldom, and that it was a weapon not to be used in the first instance, but in the last resort. He said, 'The hand should not be laid on the sword too hastily.' He used to say that when a man has no pressing reason to delay, then if he does not quickly obey an order given under obedience he neither fears God nor respects man. Neither is anything more true than this, for the authority to command in the hands of a person who uses it rashly is like a sword in the hand of an angry man. And who is more abandoned than a Religious who ignores or despises obedience?

50

How he answered friars who were persuading him to ask permission for them to preach freely.

SOME of the friars said to blessed Francis, 'Father, do you not realize that sometimes the bishops will not allow us to preach, and make us wait around idle in one place for many days before we can preach the word of God? It would be better if you sought some privilege from the Lord Pope in this matter, for it concerns the salvation of souls.'

He answered them with a stern rebuke, saying, 'You Friars Minor don't understand God's will, and won't allow me to convert the whole world in the way God wills. For first of all I want to convert the bishops by our holy humility and respect.

When they come to see our holy way of life and our humble respect for them, they will ask you to preach and convert the people. These things will draw people to your preaching far better than your privileges, which would only lead you into pride.

'And if you are free from all avarice and can persuade the people to restore their rights to the churches, they will themselves ask you to hear the confessions of their people; although you need not concern yourselves on this matter, for once they are converted, they will easily find confessors. For my part, the only favour that I ask of God is that I may never receive any favours from men. I wish to show respect to everyone, and by obedience to the holy Rule, to convert all men by my own example rather than by words.'

51

On the custom by which the friars in those days effected a reconciliation when one friar had offended another.

HE used to say that the Friars Minor had been sent by God in these latest days to set an example to those who were shrouded in the darkness of their sins. He said that whenever he heard about the great achievements of holy friars who were scattered all over the world, he was bathed in the sweetest of perfumes and anointed with the virtue of precious unguents.

On one occasion one of the friars happened to speak harshly to another in the presence of a nobleman of Cyprus. Directly he realized that his brother was somewhat distressed by this, he was angry with himself, and taking up some ass's dung, he put it in his mouth, and ground it with his teeth, saying, 'The tongue that has poured out the poison of anger against my brother shall see what dung tastes like!' The nobleman who saw this was struck with amazement, and went away much

THE PORZIUNCULA

As it remains to-day

edified; and thenceforward he placed himself and all his property at the disposal of the friars.

All the friars observed a custom that whenever any of them said anything hurtful or offensive to another, he would at once throw himself to the ground and kiss the feet of the offended brother, humbly asking his pardon. The holy Father was very happy whenever he heard that his sons were setting examples of holiness of their own accord, and he lavished most acceptable blessings on friars who brought sinners to the love of Christ by word or deed. For he desired that his sons should bear a true resemblance to him in the zeal for souls that filled him so completely.

52

How Christ complained to Brother Leo, the companion of blessed Francis, about the ingratitude and pride of the friars.

THE Lord Jesus Christ once complained to Brother Leo, the companion of blessed Francis: 'Friar Leo, I am grieved with the friars.' And Brother Leo replied, 'Why so, Lord?' And the Lord said, 'For three reasons. Firstly, because they do not recognize My blessings, which, as you know, I pour upon them so freely and abundantly, although they neither sow nor reap. Secondly, because they grumble and are idle all day long. And thirdly, because they often provoke one another to anger and do not return to love, nor do they pardon any injury that they receive.'

53

How he gave a true and humble answer to a Doctor of the Order of Preachers, who questioned him on a passage of Scripture.

WHILE he was staying in Siena he was visited by a Doctor of Theology from the Order of Preachers, a man who was both

C 63

humble and sincerely spiritual. When he had discussed the words of our Lord with blessed Francis for some while, this Doctor asked him about the passage in Ezekiel: *When I threaten the sinner with doom of death, it is for thee to give him word and warn him.* And he said, 'Good Father, I know many people who are in mortal sin, and do not warn them of their wickedness. Will their souls be required at my hand?' Blessed Francis humbly answered that he was no scholar, so that it would be more profitable for him to receive instruction from his questioner than to offer his own opinion on Scripture. The humble Doctor then added, 'Brother, although I have heard this passage expounded by various learned men, I would be glad to know how you interpret it.' So blessed Francis said, 'If the passage is to be understood in general terms, I take it to mean that a servant of God should burn and shine in such a way by his own life and holiness that he rebukes all wicked people by the light of his example and the devoutness of his conversation; in this way the brightness of his life and the fragrance of his reputation will make all men aware of their own wickedness.'

Greatly edified, the Doctor went away, and said to the companions of blessed Francis, 'My brothers, this man's theology is grounded on purity and contemplation, and resembles a flying eagle; but our knowledge crawls along the ground on its belly.'

54

On preserving humility, and on being at peace with the clergy.

BLESSED Francis wished his sons to be at peace with all men and to behave themselves humbly to everyone, but he showed them by his own words and example to be especially humble to the clergy. For he said, 'We have been sent to help the clergy in the salvation of souls, so that we may supply whatever is lacking in them. But men will not be rewarded according to their office, but their work. Remember, my brothers, that the winning of souls is what pleases God most, and we can do this better by working in harmony with the clergy than in opposition. But if they obstruct the salvation of the people, vengeance belongs to God, and He will punish them in His own time. So obey your superiors, and let there be no wrongful jealousy on your part. If you are sons of peace, you will win both clergy and people, and this will be more pleasing to God than if you were to win the people alone and alienate the clergy. Conceal their mistakes and make up for their many defects; and when you have done this, be even more humble than before.'

55

How he humbly obtained the church of S. Mary of the Angels from the Abbot of S. Benedict at Assisi, and how he wished the friars always to live there and behave with humility.

WHEN blessed Francis saw that the Lord willed to increase the number of the friars, he said to them: 'My dearest brothers and sons, I realize that God wills to add to our numbers. It seems good and godly to me that we should obtain from the Bishop, or from the Canons of S. Ruffino, or from the Abbot of S. Benedict some church where the friars may say their Hours, and have some poor little dwelling near by made of clay and wattle where the brethren may rest and work. For this place is not suitable or adequate for the friars now that the Lord wills to increase our numbers, especially as we have no church here where the friars can say their Hours. And if any friar were to die, it would not be fitting to bury him here or in a church belonging to the secular clergy.' And all the friars supported this suggestion.

So he went to the Bishop of Assisi and put this request to him. But the Bishop said, 'Brother, I have no church to offer you,' and the Canons gave the same answer. Then he went to the Abbot of S. Benedict on Monte Subasio, and made the

65

same request to him. The Abbot was roused to sympathy, and took counsel with his monks; and guided by the grace and will of God, he granted to blessed Francis and his friars the church of S. Mary of the Porziuncula, which was the smallest and poorest church that they had. And the Abbot said to blessed Francis, 'See, Brother, we have granted your request. But if the Lord causes this congregation of yours to grow, we wish this place to become the chief of all your churches.' His suggestion pleased blessed Francis and his brethren, and he was delighted with this place granted to the friars, especially since the church was named after the Mother of Christ, and was so poor and small. He was also happy that it was called the *Porziuncula*, which foreshadowed that it was destined to become the Mother-House and chief church of the poor Friars Minor, for it had been known by this name from earliest times. So blessed Francis used to say, 'This was why the Lord willed that no other church should be given to the friars, and that the first friars should not build a new church or have any but this'; for in this way an old prophecy was fulfilled by the coming of the Friars Minor. And although it was poor and nearly in ruins, the people of the city of Assisi and the whole district had for a long time held the church in great reverence. To-day their reverence is still greater, and grows day by day.

So the friars at once went to live there, and the Lord added to their numbers almost daily. And the fragrance of their reputation spread marvellously through the Vale of Spoleto and many parts of the land. But in ancient times it had been called S. Mary of the Angels, because it was said that the songs of angels were often heard there.

Although the Abbot and monks had made a free gift of the church to blessed Francis and his friars, he, as a good and experienced master-builder, wished to establish his house—that is, his Order—on a firm foundation of absolute poverty. So each year he sent to the Abbot and monks a basket or jar full of little fish, known as *lasche*. This served as a reminder of their greater poverty and humility, and of the fact that the friars were to possess no place of their own, or live in any place that was not the property of others, so that the friars had no right to buy or sell anything. But when the friars carried the fish to the monks each year, the monks used to give them a jar of oil, in recognition of the humility of blessed Francis who had done this of his own free will.

Those of us who lived with blessed Francis testify that he solemnly affirmed that it had been revealed to him that the Blessed Virgin had a greater love for this church than for any others in the world, because of the many favours that God had granted there. So thenceforward he held it in the greatest reverence and devotion; and in order that the friars should always remember this in their hearts, he had it written in his Testament at his death that all friars should do likewise. For about the time of his death he said in the presence of the Minister General and other friars: 'I wish to entrust and bequeath the friary of S. Mary of the Porziuncula to my brethren by my Testament, in order that it may always be held in the greatest reverence and devotion by the friars. Our earliest brethren always did this, and because this place is holy, beloved, and chosen before all others by Christ and the glorious Virgin, they preserved its sanctity by constant prayer and silence day and night. If they had occasion to speak after the close of the appointed silence, they did so with the greatest devotion and sincerity, and only on matters which concerned the praise of God and the salvation of souls. And if ever anyone began to talk unprofitably or idly—although this seldom occurred—he was at once corrected by another friar.

'These brethren used to discipline their bodies with many fasts and vigils, with cold, nakedness, and manual labour. To avoid idleness they often helped the poor in their fields, and afterwards gave them the bread of the love of God. They hallowed the place with these and other virtues, and kept themselves in sanctity. But since those days, because friars and layfolk visit the place more often than before, and because the friars are less zealous in prayer and good works, and are more undisciplined in engaging in idle conversation and discussing worldly events than they used to be, the place is not held in so great a reverence and devotion as was customary hitherto, and as I would wish it to be.'

Having said this, he ended with great fervour, saying, 'I wish this place always to be under the direct control of the Minister General and servant, so that he may exercise the greatest care and responsibility in providing a good and holy family for it. The clergy are to be chosen from among the better, more holy, and more suitable of the friars, who best know how to recite the Office and who are fully professed in the Order, so that both layfolk and the other friars may see and hear them gladly and with great devotion. The lay-brothers chosen to serve them are to be holy men, discreet, humble and honest. I do not wish anyone else, whether layfolk or friars, to enter the place, except the Minister General and the lay-brothers who serve them. The friars themselves are not to speak to anyone except the brothers who serve them and the Minister General when he visits them. Similarly, the lay-brothers who serve them are never to gossip with them or tell them worldly news, or anything that is not of benefit to their souls. I particularly desire that no one else shall enter this place, so that its purity and holiness may the better be preserved, and that nothing un-edifying be done or said there. Let the whole place be kept pure and holy with hymns and praises to God.

'And whenever any of the friars shall pass away to the Lord, I wish the Minister General to send a holy friar from another house to take his place. For even if other friars have at times fallen away from purity and sincerity, I wish this place to be blessed, and to remain for ever as a mirror and holy pattern for the whole Order, and as a lamp burning and shining before the throne of God and of the Blessed Virgin. For the sake of this place may God pardon the defects and faults of all the friars, and protect this Order, His little plant, for ever.'

56

On the humble reverence which he showed by sweeping and cleaning churches.

ONCE while he was staying at S. Mary of the Porziuncula and there were as yet few friars, blessed Francis went through the villages and churches round about the city of Assisi proclaiming and preaching to the people that they should do penance. And he carried a broom to sweep out churches that were dirty, for he was very grieved when he found any church not as clean as he wished.

So when he had ended his sermon, he would always gather all the priests in some private place so that he would not be overheard by layfolk, and speak to them about the salvation of souls, stressing in particular how they should take care to keep the churches and altars clean, as well as everything that concerned the celebration of the Divine Mysteries.

57

On the peasant who found him humbly sweeping a church; how the man was converted, entered the Order, and became a holy friar.

ONCE blessed Francis went to a village church in the neighbourhood of Assisi, and humbly began to sweep and clean it. A report of what he was doing immediately spread through the whole village, for the people were always happy to see him and even more happy to listen to him. But when a peasant named John, a man of wonderful simplicity, heard about it as he was ploughing in his field, he went to him at once and found him humbly and devoutly sweeping the church. And he said to him, 'Brother, give me the broom; I would like to help you.' And taking the broom from his hands, he swept the rest of the church.

While they were sitting down together, he said to blessed Francis, 'Brother, I have longed to serve God for a long time, especially since I have heard accounts of you and your friars, but I did not know how to find you. Now that it has pleased God that I should see you, I would like to do whatever you think best.' Recognizing his fervour, the blessed Father gave thanks to God, for at that time he had few brethren, and it seemed that the man's simplicity and purity would make him a good Religious. So he said to him, 'Brother, if you wish to join our life and society, you will have to strip yourself of all that you possess, so far as is right, and give it to the poor as the holy Gospel teaches. For all my friars who could do so have done the same.'

Hearing this, the peasant at once went back to the field where he had left his oxen and untied them. And he led one of them to blessed Francis, saying, 'Brother, I have served my father and family for many years, and although my part of the inheritance is small, I would like to take this ox as my share, and give it to the poor as you think best.' But when his parents and brothers, who were still small, realized that he intended to leave them, they began to weep aloud, and uttered such pitiful cries of grief that blessed Francis was moved to compassion, for the family was large and they were simple folk. He said: 'Prepare a meal for us all, and let us eat together. And don't weep, because I am going to make you really happy.' So they prepared it at once, and all ate together with great joy.

After the meal blessed Francis said to them, 'This son of yours wishes to serve God, and you ought not to be grieved at this, but very glad. It will bring you great honour and blessing in soul and body, both in the eyes of God and those of the world, for God will be honoured by your own flesh and blood, and all our friars will become your sons and brothers. I cannot and may not return your son to you, for he is God's creature and wishes to serve his Creator, to serve whom is to reign. But in order to console you I want him to give you this ox as he would do to the poor, although he should have given it to other poor folk as the Gospel teaches.' And they were all comforted by the words of blessed Francis, and overjoyed that the ox was restored to them, for they were very poor.

And because blessed Francis took the greatest delight in pure and holy simplicity, whether in himself or others, he immediately clothed Brother John in the religious habit and humbly took him as his own companion. Now John was so simple that he thought himself obliged to copy everything that blessed Francis did. So whenever blessed Francis stood to pray in church or anywhere else, he wanted to watch him so that he could follow his every movement. And if blessed Francis knelt, or raised his hands to heaven, or spat, or sighed, he did the same. When the Father noticed this, he took him to task with great amusement for simplicity of this sort. But he answered, 'Brother, I have promised to do everything that you do, so I must imitate you in all things.' And blessed Francis was amazed and very pleased to find him so pure and simple.

In due course Brother John made such progress in all virtues and good ways that blessed Francis and all the friars marvelled at his perfection. And after a few years he died in this state of holy virtue, and in later days blessed Francis used to tell the friars about his conversion with great joy, and spoke of him, not as Brother John, but as holy John.

58

How he punished himself by eating out of the same dish as a leper, because he had caused him humiliation.

WHEN blessed Francis had returned to the church of S. Mary of the Porziuncula, he found Brother James the Simple there with a leper who was covered with sores. For blessed Francis had entrusted this leper and all the others to his care, because he was like a doctor to them, and gladly handled their wounds, changed the dressings, and looked after them, for at that time the friars used to live in the leper-hospice.

Blessed Francis reproved Brother James, saying, 'You should not take our brothers in Christ about in this way; it is not fitting for you or for them.' For although he wished to serve them, he did not want him to take those who were badly diseased outside the hospice, because people looked on them with such revulsion. But Brother James was so simple that he used to go with them from the hospice as far as the church of S. Mary, as though he was walking with the friars. And blessed Francis himself used to call the lepers 'brothers in Christ.'

As soon as he had uttered these words, blessed Francis reproached himself, feeling that the leper had been put to humiliation by the rebuke given to Brother James. So wishing to make amends to God and the leper, he confessed his fault to Peter Catanii, who was Minister General at the time. And he said, 'I wish you to confirm the penance that I have chosen to do for this fault, and ask you not to oppose me in any way.' 'Do as you wish, Brother,' he replied. For Brother Peter so venerated and feared him that he would not presume to oppose him, although he often had cause to regret it.

Then blessed Francis said, 'This is to be my penance: I am going to eat out of the same dish as my brother in Christ.' So when he sat down at table with the leper, a single dish was placed between blessed Francis and the leper. Now the leper was covered in sores and repulsive, especially as the fingers with which he took pieces of food from the dish were shrivelled and bleeding, so that when he placed them in the dish blood and matter dripped into it. Brother Peter and the other friars were greatly shocked as they watched this, but dared not say anything because of their fear and reverence for the holy Father.

The writer saw these things himself, and testifies to them.

How he put devils to flight by humble prayer.

BLESSED Francis once visited the church of S. Peter of Bovara near the castle of Trevi in the Vale of Spoleto, and with him went Brother Pacificus, who in the world had been known as 'The King of Verse,' a nobleman and master of singers at the Court. But the church was deserted, and blessed Francis said to Brother Pacificus, 'Go back to the leper-hospice, for I would like to remain alone here to-night; but come back for me very early to-morrow.'

So he remained there by himself, and when he had said Compline and other prayers, he wished to rest and sleep, but could not do so, for his soul grew afraid, his body trembled, and he began to experience diabolic temptations. So making the sign of the Cross he immediately left the church, saying, 'In the Name of Almighty God, I tell you devils that you may do to my body whatever our Lord Jesus Christ allows, for I am ready to endure anything. My own body is the worst enemy that I have, so that you will be taking vengeance on my own adversary and direst foe.' At once these temptations ceased, and when he had returned to the place where he had been lying, he fell into a peaceful sleep.

On the vision seen by Brother Pacificus, and how he heard that the seat of Lucifer was reserved for the humble Francis.

EARLY next morning Brother Pacificus returned and found blessed Francis standing before the altar in prayer. So he waited for him outside the choir, and himself prayed before the crucifix. And as he began to pray, he was caught up into heaven—whether his spirit left his body I cannot tell—and saw many thrones set in heaven. One of these was more exalted and glorious than all others, adorned and glowing with all kinds of precious stones. As he admired its beauty, he began to wonder whose throne it might be; when all at once he heard a voice saying to him, 'This was the throne of Lucifer, and the humble Francis shall sit on it in his place.'

As soon as he returned to himself, blessed Francis came out to him, and immediately Brother Pacificus fell at his feet, folding his arms in the form of a cross. And gazing at him as though he were already seated on that throne in heaven, he said to him, 'Father, hear my petition, and ask God to have mercy on me and forgive my sins.' But blessed Francis stretched out his hand and raised him, knowing inwardly that Brother Pacificus had seen some vision during his prayer, for he seemed quite altered, and spoke to him not as though he were living in the body, but already reigning in heaven. And Brother Pacificus was unwilling to talk about his vision afterwards, but began to speak of other things. Later he said, 'Brother, what do you think of yourself?' And blessed Francis replied, 'I think that I am a greater sinner than anyone in this world.' And at once it came to the mind of Brother Pacificus, 'By this sign you can be sure that the vision that you have seen is true. For as Lucifer was cast down from that throne because of his pride, so blessed Francis will merit to be raised up and take his place on it because of his humility.'

61

How blessed Francis had himself led naked before the people with a rope tied round his neck.

ONCE when he had recovered somewhat from a very grave illness, he felt that he had been rather self-indulgent during it, although in fact he had eaten very little. So although not yet recovered from quartan fever, he got up one day and had the people of the town of Assisi called together in the square for a sermon. But after the sermon he asked the people not to leave the place until he returned. And he went into the Cathedral of S. Ruffino with many of the friars, and with Brother Peter Catanii, who had been a canon of that church and was chosen as the first Minister General by blessed Francis. And he ordered Brother Peter under obedience to do whatever he told him without argument. Brother Peter answered, 'Brother, I neither may or should desire anything or do anything either on your behalf or my own without your permission.'

Then blessed Francis removed his habit, and told Brother Peter to fasten a cord round his neck and lead him naked in front of the people to the place where he had preached to them. He told another friar to take a bowl of ashes, and go up to the place where he had preached; and when they arrived, he was to throw the ashes in his face. This friar did not obey him, because of the deep compassion and pity that he had for him; but Brother Peter, however, took the cord fastened round his neck, and led him along as he had ordered. And as he went he wept aloud, and the other friars with him shed tears of compassion and grief.

When blessed Francis had been led naked before the people to the place where he had preached, he said to them, 'You, and all who have followed me in renouncing the world and entered the Order and life of the Friars, believe me to be a holy man. But I confess before God and you that during my illness I have eaten meat and stew flavoured with meat.' In their great devotion and pity for him, most of the people began to weep, especially as it was winter and bitterly cold, and he had not yet recovered from quartan fever. And they beat their breasts, accusing themselves, and saying, 'We know that this saint leads a holy life, for he has reduced his body to the likeness of a living corpse by his abstinence and austerity ever since his conversion to Christ. And if he accuses himself with such remorse for having taken what was right and necessary for his body, what shall we wretches do, who have spent our entire lives gratifying the desires of the flesh, and still do so?'

62

How he wanted everyone to know what comforts his body had enjoyed.

ON another occasion, while he was living in a certain hermitage (*Poggio Bustone*) during the Fast of S. Martin (*November* 11 *until the Eve of Christmas*), he had eaten some food cooked in lard, because oil was very bad for him in his weakness. At the end of the fast, as he was preaching to a great crowd of people, the opening words of his sermon were, 'You have come to me with great devotion, supposing me to be a holy man; but I confess before God and you that during this fast I have eaten food cooked in lard.'

Whenever he was eating with layfolk, or when some delicacy had been prepared by the friars because of his weakness, he would usually publish the fact both inside and outside the house in front of any friars and layfolk who did not know about it, saying, 'I have eaten such and such food,' for he did not wish to conceal from man what was known to God. In the same way, in whatever place or company his spirit was tempted to pride, vainglory, or any other sin, he at once confessed it to them openly and without concealment. On one occasion he said to his companions, 'In any hermitage or other place where I stay I wish to live as though everyone could see me; for if they think me a holy man and I do not lead a life becoming to a holy man, I shall be a hypocrite.'

When it was bitterly cold and one of his companions, who was his Guardian, wanted to sew a small piece of fox fur under his habit to protect his weak stomach and spleen, blessed Francis said, 'If you want me to wear fox fur under my habit, I must wear a piece of fur outside, so that everyone may know that I am wearing it underneath as well.' So he had it made in this way; but although it was very necessary to him, he seldom wore it.

How he accused himself of vainglory directly he had given alms.

WHILE he was walking through the town of Assisi, a poor old woman asked alms of him for the love of God, and he immediately gave her the cloak from his back. And forthwith he confessed to those following him that he had felt vainglory in doing so.

We have seen and heard so many other similar instances of his sublime humility that we who knew him well cannot relate them all, either in words or writing. But blessed Francis's chief concern was that he should not be a hypocrite in the eyes of God. And although dispensations were often essential because of his infirmities, he felt that he must always set a good example to the friars and to others; so he patiently endured every privation in order to remove all grounds for criticism.

How he described the state of perfect humility in his own case.

WHEN the time of the Chapter was approaching, blessed Francis said to his companion, 'It seems to me that I would not be a true Friar Minor unless I were in the state that I will describe to you. Suppose that the friars invite me to the Chapter with great respect and devotion, and touched by their devotion, I go to the Chapter with them. During the assembly they ask me to proclaim the word of God and preach before them, so I rise and preach to them as the Holy Spirit moves me. Suppose that after my sermon they all cry out against me, saying, "We will not have you ruling over us! You have not the necessary eloquence, and you are too stupid and simple. We are very ashamed to have such a simple and contemptible Superior over us; henceforward do not presume to call yourself our Superior!" So they depose me with abuse and contempt. It seems to me that I would not be a true Friar Minor unless I were just as happy when they abused me and deposed me in disgrace, unwilling that I should remain their Superior, as when they held me in respect and honour, for in either case their welfare and usefulness is my first desire. For if I was happy when they praised and honoured me in their devotion—which may well be a danger to my soul—I ought to rejoice and be far happier at the benefit and health brought to my soul when they abuse me, for this is a sure spiritual gain.'

65

How he humbly desired to visit distant Provinces, as he had sent other friars; and how he instructed the friars to go through the world humbly and devoutly.

AT the end of the Chapter, when many friars were sent to a number of Provinces overseas, blessed Francis remained behind with some of the friars. And he said to them, 'Dearest Brothers, it is my duty to provide a pattern and example to all the friars. So, as I have sent friars to distant lands to endure toil and abuse, hunger and thirst, and other hardships, it is only right, and holy humility requires, that I should likewise go to some distant Province. When the brethren hear that I am undergoing the same trials as they, they will bear their own hardships all the more patiently. So go and pray God that He will guide me to choose the Province where I can best labour to His glory, to the benefit of souls, and be a good example to our Order.'

For whenever the most holy Father intended to go to any Province, he would first pray, and send the friars to ask God that He would guide his heart to go to whatever place was most pleasing to Him. And at once he said to them with joy, 'In the Name of our Lord Jesus Christ, of the glorious Virgin His Mother, and of all the Saints, I choose the Province of France, for it is a Catholic nation, and they show an especial reverence to the Body of Christ above other Catholics. This is a great joy to me, and because of this I will most gladly live among them.'

Blessed Francis had such great reverence and devotion to the Body of Christ that he caused it to be written in the Rule that in every Province where the friars lived, they were to give much thought and care to this matter, and to plead with priests to reserve the Body of Christ in worthy and fitting places; and if they neglected this, the friars were to do it themselves.

He also wished it to be included in the Rule that wherever friars found the Name of our Lord or the words by which the Body of Christ is consecrated lying about in unseemly places, they were to gather them up and lay them in a seemly place, and by so doing honour our Lord in His words. And although he did not write this in the Rule because the Ministers did not think that the friars ought to be compelled to do this, he made his wishes clear to the friars on this matter in his Testament and other writings. Indeed, at one time he wished to send friars through all the Provinces carrying fair clean pyxes, and wherever they found the Lord's Body reserved unworthily, they were to place It in these pyxes with all honour. He also wanted to send friars through all Provinces with good new wafer-irons to make fine pure hosts.

When blessed Francis had chosen the friars he wished to take with him, he said to them, 'Take the road two and two in the Name of the Lord. Be humble and sincere. Keep silence from dawn until after Terce, praying to God in your hearts, and do not indulge in idle and unprofitable conversation. Although you are travelling, let your words be as humble and devout as in a hermitage or cell. For wherever we are, or wherever we go, we always take our cell with us; for Brother Body is our cell, and our soul is the hermit who lives in it, constantly praying to God and meditating on Him. If the soul cannot remain quiet in its cell, then a cell made with hands is of little value to a Religious.'

When he arrived in Florence, blessed Francis found there the Lord Ugolino, Bishop of Ostia, who later became Pope Gregory. When the Cardinal heard from blessed Francis that he proposed to go to France, he forbade it, saying, 'Brother, I do not want you to cross the Alps, for there are many prelates who would willingly damage the prospects of your Order at the Roman Court. But I and other Cardinals who love your Order will protect and support it all the more willingly if you remain within this Province.'

Blessed Francis answered the Cardinal, 'My Lord, I should be very ashamed if I sent my brothers to distant Provinces, while I remained here without sharing any of the hardships that they have to suffer for God's sake.' As though in reproof, the Lord Cardinal said to him, 'Why have you sent your friars to such distant places to die of hunger and undergo other hardships?' Moved by the spirit of prophecy, blessed Francis replied with deep fervour, 'My Lord, do you imagine that God has raised up the friars solely for the benefit of these Provinces? I solemnly assure you that God has chosen and sent the friars for the benefit and salvation of the souls of all men in this world. They will be welcomed not only in the countries of the faithful, but in those of unbelievers as well, and they will win many souls.'

The Lord Bishop of Ostia wondered at his words, and admitted that he spoke the truth. And because he would not allow him to go to France, blessed Francis sent Brother Pacificus and many other friars, while he himself returned to the Vale of Spoleto.

How he showed the friars how to win the souls of some bandits by humility and charity.

A PARTY of bandits who used to hide in the woods and rob travellers occasionally came for food to a hermitage of the friars situated above Borgo San Sepolcro. Some of the friars said that it was not right to give them alms, while others did so out of compassion, and urged them to repent. Meanwhile blessed Francis came to this friary, and the brothers asked him whether it was right to give them alms. And he said to them, 'If you will do as I tell you, I trust in God that we shall win their souls. So go and bring some good bread and wine, and take it to the woods where they live. And shout to them, saying, "Brother bandits, come to us. We are friars, and are bringing you some good bread and wine!" And they will come at once. Then you must spread a cloth on the ground, place the bread and wine on it, and serve them humbly and gladly until they have eaten. After the meal speak to them of our Lord's words, and end by asking them for the love of God to grant your first request, which is to promise not to strike or injure anyone. For if you ask for everything at once, they will not listen to you; but because you are humble and loving they will promise this immediately. On a later day take them eggs and cheese with the bread and wine to show that you appreciate their promise, and serve them until they have eaten. And after the meal say to them, "Why do you stay here all day to die of hunger, and suffer so much hardship? And why do you do so many evil things, for which you will lose your souls unless you turn to God? It is better to serve God, for He will both supply your bodily needs in this world, and save your souls at the last." Then God will move them to repentance because of the humility and charity that you have shown them.'

So the friars did everything that blessed Francis had told

them, and by the grace and mercy of God the bandits listened to them, and punctiliously observed all that the friars had humbly asked of them. Further, because of the friars' humility and friendship towards them, they themselves humbly began to serve the friars and carried logs up to the hermitage on their shoulders for them. At length some of the bandits entered the Order; the others confessed their crimes and did penance for their sins, laying their hands in those of the friars, and promising that henceforward they would live by their own labour and never do such things again.

67

How he was beaten by devils, and thus knew that God was better pleased when he stayed in poor and humble places than with Cardinals.

BLESSED Francis once went to Rome to visit the Lord Cardinal of Ostia. And when he had stayed with him for some days, he visited the Lord Cardinal Leo, who was greatly attached to him. Because it was winter, and utterly unfit for travelling on foot because of the cold, wind and rain, Cardinal Leo invited him to stay with him for a few days, and to receive his food from him as a beggar at the same time as other beggars who used to eat in his house every day. He said this because he knew that whenever blessed Francis was offered hospitality, he always wished to be treated as a beggar, although the Lord Pope and Cardinals welcomed him with the greatest devotion and reverence, and venerated him as a saint. And he added, 'If you wish, I will give you a good secluded house where you can pray and have your food.' Then Friar Angelo Tancredi, who was one of the first twelve friars and was also staying with the Cardinal, said to blessed Francis, 'Brother, near here is a spacious and secluded tower, where you could live as though in a hermitage.' When blessed Francis had seen it, he was pleased with it, and returning to the Lord Cardinal, he said, 'My Lord, perhaps I will remain with you for some days.' And the Cardinal was delighted. So Brother Angelo went and prepared a place in the tower for blessed Francis and his companion. And because he did not wish to leave the tower during his stay with the Cardinal, Brother Angelo promised to bring up food to him and his companion each day.

During the first night after blessed Francis had gone there with his companion, when he wished to sleep devils came and gave him a violent beating. Calling to his companion, he said, 'Brother, devils have been giving me a violent beating; I would like you to stay with me, for I am afraid to remain alone.' And his companion stayed near him that night, for blessed Francis shook like a man with fever, so that both of them remained awake the whole night. Meanwhile blessed Francis said to his companion, 'Why have the devils beaten me? And why has God given them power to hurt me?' And he went on, 'The devils are God's constables, for just as the authorities send a constable to punish a wrong-doer, so does God correct and punish those whom He loves through the devils who are His constables and act as His servants in this office. Even a perfect Religious often sins in ignorance; consequently, if he does not realize his sin, he is punished by the devil so that he may realize and carefully consider how he may have sinned, whether inwardly or outwardly. For in this life God leaves nothing unpunished in those whom He loves with a tender love. By the mercy and grace of God, I do not know whether I have offended Him in any way for which I have not atoned by confession and satisfaction. Indeed, God in His mercy has granted me the favour to receive in my prayer a clear knowledge of any way in which I please or displease Him. Perhaps He is now punishing me through His constables because, although the Lord Cardinal was glad to do me a kindness, and although rest is necessary to my body, my brethren who go through the world suffering hunger and many hardships, and other brethren who live in squalid little huts, may have grounds for complaint against me

83

when they hear that I am lodging with a cardinal. They may say, "We are enduring many hardships while he is living in luxury!" But I am always obliged to set a good example, and this is why I was given to them. For the friars are more edified when I live among them in their poor little huts than when I live elsewhere; and they bear their own difficulties all the more patiently when they hear that I am bearing the same.'

It was always the chief and constant concern of our Father to set a good example to us all, and to avoid any occasion for complaint from other friars. Because of this, whether in health or sickness, he suffered so greatly that whenever friars who knew him intimately—as did we who were with him until the day of his death—read of or recall these sufferings, they cannot restrain their tears, and they all bear their own troubles and privations with greater patience and joy.

So blessed Francis came down from the tower very early in the morning, and going to the Lord Cardinal, told him all that had happened and what he and his companion had endured. And he said to him, 'People think that I am a holy man, but devils have driven me out of the tower!' And although the Cardinal was delighted to have him, he knew and reverenced him as a Saint, and did not wish to oppose him once he had become unwilling to remain there. So blessed Francis bade him farewell, and returned to the hermitage of Fonte Colombo, near Rieti.

68

How he rebuked friars who wanted to follow the path of prudence and learning and not of humility; and how he foretold the reform and restoration of the Order to its early state.

WHEN blessed Francis was at the Chapter General held at S. Mary of the Porziuncula—known as the Chapter of Mats, because the only shelters there consisted of rush-mats, which were used by five thousand friars—a number of prudent and learned friars went to the Lord Cardinal of Ostia who was present, and said to him, 'My Lord, we wish that you would persuade Brother Francis to follow the advice of the wiser brethren, and allow himself to be guided by them.' And they quoted the Rules of Saint Benedict, Saint Augustine, and Saint Bernard, which lay down the principles of the regular life.

The Cardinal repeated all that they had said to blessed Francis in the form of advice; but without making any answer he took the Cardinal by the hand and led him before the friars assembled in Chapter. And he spoke to the friars in the fervour and power of the Holy Spirit, saying, 'My brothers! my brothers! God has called me by the way of simplicity and humility, and has in truth revealed this way for me and for all who are willing to trust and follow me. So I do not want you to quote any other Rule to me, whether that of Saint Benedict, Saint Augustine, or Saint Bernard, or to recommend any other way or form of life except this way which God in His mercy has revealed and given to me. The Lord told me that He wished me to be a new kind of simpleton in this world, and He does not wish us to live by any other wisdom but this. God will confound you through your own prudence and learning. And I trust in the constables of God, that He will punish you through them. Eventually, whether you wish it or not, you will return with great remorse to your first state.'

The Cardinal was utterly dumbfounded and said nothing; and all the friars were filled with great fear.

69

How he foresaw and predicted that learning would bring disaster on the Order, and how he forbade one of his friars to study the science of preaching.

BLESSED Francis was very grieved whenever he found virtue neglected in favour of the sort of learning that brings pride, especially if anyone was not persevering in the vocation to which he had first been called. He used to say, 'Friars of mine who are seduced by a desire for learning will find their hands empty in the day of trouble. I would rather have them grow stronger in virtue, so that when the time of trial comes, they will have God with them in their struggle. For a troublous time is coming when books will be no good for anything, and will be cast aside in windows and corners.'

He did not say this because the study of Holy Scripture displeased him, but to restrain all the friars from a useless preoccupation with learning. He would rather have them excel in charity than in strange forms of knowledge. He already sensed that before long a time was coming when the corrupting influence of learning would bring disaster. He therefore appeared after his death to one of the friars who was over engrossed in the study of preaching to rebuke and forbid him. And he ordered him to study how to walk in the way of humility and simplicity.

70

How those who were to enter the Order in the coming time of trouble would be blessed, and those who were tested would be better than their predecessors.

BLESSED Francis used to say, 'The time is coming when this Order, so dear to God, will be brought into such disrepute by the bad example of evil friars that its members will be ashamed to appear in public. But those who come to receive the habit of the Order in those days will be guided solely by the workings of the Holy Spirit: flesh and blood will not contaminate them, and they will be truly blessed by God. And although no noble works will be done by them because the love that enables the Saints to labour so fervently will have grown cold, they will be assailed by tremendous temptations. But those who are found worthy in those days will be better friars than their predecessors.

'But woe to those who maintain only an outward show and pretence of the Religious Life, who congratulate themselves, trusting in their own cleverness and knowledge, and are shown to be good for nothing. For they do not devote themselves to good works in the way of the Cross and of penitence, nor in the honest observance of the Gospel which their profession binds them to observe purely and simply. Men like these will not stoutly resist the temptations which God allows to test His chosen; but those who have been tried and approved will receive the crown of life, and the evil lives of the apostates will only spur them to greater efforts.'

71

Saint Francis's answer to a friar who asked why he did not correct the abuses that occurred in the Order in his own time.

ONE of blessed Francis's companions once said to him, 'Father, forgive me, but I would like to speak to you about something that several of us have recently been discussing.' He went on, 'You know how in earlier days, by the grace of God, the whole Order flourished in the purity of perfection; how all the friars were loyal to holy Poverty in all things with great fervour and strictness, in such things as small and humble dwellings and furnishings, and in few and poor books and clothes. Furthermore, they had a common purpose and zeal in all outward things, and carefully observed all the obligations proper to our profession and vocation, and which are intended for the edification of all. So they were united in the love of God and their neighbour, and were truly apostolic and evangelical men.

'But for some while now this purity and perfection has begun to decline, although many offer as an excuse the great number of the friars, saying that this is why they cannot observe this ideal.

Furthermore, many friars have become so blind as to imagine that people will be edified and turned to devotion by their present ways rather than by the former, and they imagine that they are living more sensibly in this way. They despise and disregard the way of holy simplicity and poverty, which is the first principle and foundation of our Order. So we have been considering these things, and are quite certain that they are displeasing to you. But if they displease you, we cannot understand why you tolerate them and do not correct them.'

Blessed Francis answered, 'Brother, God forgive you for wanting to criticize and oppose me, and to involve me in matters which no longer concern my office. As long as I held a position of authority over the friars, and they persevered in their vocation and profession, they were content with my feeble care, example and preaching, although from the beginning of my conversion I had always been a sick man. But later I considered how the Lord had added to the number of the friars, and how, through lukewarmness and lack of zeal, they were beginning to turn aside from the right and sure way by which they had once walked. They entered on the broader way that leads to death, and did not hold to their vocation and profession, nor were they willing to abandon this perilous and deadly road, despite my constant preaching, warning and example. Because of this I surrendered the rule and direction of the Order to God and the Ministers. But when I resigned the office of Superior, I explained to the brethren in General Chapter that my infirmities would no longer allow me to have charge of them. Yet, were they willing to live in accordance with my intentions, I would not wish them to have any other Minister but myself to comfort and help them until the day of my death. For once a good and faithful subject knows and obeys the will of his superior, the latter need have little anxiety about him. Indeed, I would be so happy at the good progress of the brethren—both on their own account and my own—that even if I were lying ill in bed I would not feel ashamed to fulfil this office for them, for the duties of a superior are entirely spiritual; that is, to overcome, correct and amend their faults by spiritual means. But since I am not able to correct and amend these things by my preaching, advice and example, I am not willing to become an executioner, and use punishment and flogging like the authorities of this world. I trust in the Lord that the unseen enemies of the friars, who are God's constables, will punish them in this life and the life to come, until they have taken vengeance on those who transgress His commandments and the vows of their profession. I hope that they will be reproached by the men of this world to their shame and disgrace, and as a result will return to their vocation and profession.

'However, to the day of my death I will not cease to teach the brethren by my own good example and actions to follow the way which God has shown me, and which I have taught to them by word and example. So they will have no excuse to plead before God, and I shall not be summoned to account for them before God.'

Here follows the account which Brother Leo, the companion and confessor of blessed Francis, wrote down for Brother Conrad of Offida at San Damiano near Assisi, saying that he had it from the mouth of Saint Francis himself.

While blessed Francis was standing in prayer behind the pulpit in the church of S. Mary of the Angels with his hands upraised to heaven, he called upon Christ to have mercy on the people in the great troubles which were bound to come. And the Lord said, 'Francis, if you wish Me to have mercy on the Christian people, do this for Me: see that your Order remains in the state in which it was founded, for nothing but this will remain to Me in the whole world. And I promise you that, for love of you and your Order, I will not allow any troubles to come upon the world. But I warn you that the friars will turn back from this way in which I have set them, and will provoke Me to such anger that I shall rise up against them. And I shall summon the devils, and grant them all the power that they have desired; and they will stir up such antagonism between the friars and the world that no friar will be able to wear the habit of your Order except in the woods. And when the world loses its faith, no light will remain save that of your Order, because I have set it as a light to the world.'

And blessed Francis said, 'How will my brethren survive when they live in the woods?' And Christ said, 'I shall feed them as I fed the Children of Israel with manna in the desert, for they will be good like them; and they will return to the original state in which your Order was founded and begun.'

72

How souls are converted by the prayers and tears of the humble and simple brethren, when they seem to be converted by the learning and preaching of others.

THE most holy Father did not wish his friars to hanker after learning and books, but taught them to build their lives on holy humility, to practise pure simplicity and devout prayer, and to love Lady Poverty, on which the Saints and first friars had established themselves. He used to say that this was the only sure road to their own salvation and the edification of others, because Christ, Whom we are called to follow, showed and taught us this way alone by His own teaching and example.

Looking into the future, the blessed Father knew through the Holy Spirit, and often told the friars, that in the hope of edifying others, many would abandon their vocation, which is holy humility, pure simplicity, prayer and devotion, and the love of Lady Poverty. He said, 'Because they will think themselves more gifted, more filled with devotion, fired with love, and enlightened by divine knowledge through their study of the

Scriptures, that they will as a result remain inwardly cold and empty. Consequently, they will be unable to return to their first vocation, because they will have wasted the time when they should have been following this vocation in useless and misguided study. I fear that even the grace that they seemed to possess will be taken away from them, because they have completely neglected the grace that had been given them, which is to hold to and follow their true vocation.'

He also said, 'There are many brethren who devote all their energy and zeal to the acquisition of learning, neglecting their holy vocation, and straying from the way of humility and holy prayer both in mind and body. When they have preached to the people, and learn that some have been helped or moved to penitence, they grow conceited and congratulate themselves as though the others' gain were their own. But they will have preached rather to their own condemnation and hurt, and have really achieved nothing except as the instruments of those through whom God has obtained this result. For those whom they imagined they were edifying and converting through their own learning and preaching have been edified and converted by God Himself through the prayers and tears of holy, poor, humble and simple brethren, although these holy men are not aware of it. For it is the will of God that they should know nothing of it, lest they become proud.

'These friars are my Knights of the Round Table, who remain hidden in deserts and lonely places in order to devote themselves more completely to prayer and meditation, lamenting their own sins and the sins of others, living simply and behaving humbly, whose sanctity is known to God, and at times to other friars, but unknown to the world. When the angels present their souls before God, He will show them the fruit and reward of their labours, namely, the many souls that have been saved by their prayers and tears. And He will say to them, "My dear sons, these souls have been saved by your prayers, tears, and example, and *since you have been faithful over little things, I have great things*

91

to commit to your charge. Other men have preached and laboured with their words of wisdom and learning, but through your merits, I have brought about the fruit of salvation. So receive the reward of your labours and the fruit of your merits, which is an everlasting kingdom gained by your humility and simplicity, and by the power of your prayers and tears." And *bearing their sheaves with them,* that is, the fruit and merit of their holy humility and simplicity, these holy brethren will enter into the joy of the Lord with joy and exultation.

'But those who have cared for nothing except to know and point out the way of salvation to others, and have made no effort to follow it themselves, will stand naked and empty-handed before the judgement-seat of Christ, bearing only the sheaves of confusion, shame, and grief. Then shall truth of holy humility and simplicity, of holy prayer and poverty, which is our vocation, be exalted, glorified, and proclaimed; the truth which those who were swollen with the wind of their learning betrayed by their own lives and by the words of their empty learning, saying that truth was falsehood, and blindly and cruelly persecuting those who walked in the truth. In that day the error and falsity of the opinions in which they lived—which they proclaimed as truth, and by which they have thrust many people into a pit of darkness—will be finally exposed in grief, confusion, and shame. And they themselves, together with their misguided opinions, will be *cast into outer darkness* with the spirits of darkness.'

Commenting on the passage, *See how at last the barren womb bears many, and the fruitful mother is left to languish,* blessed Francis used to say, 'The barren represents the good Religious, simple, humble, poor, and despised, who edifies others at all times by his holy prayers and virtues, and brings forth fruit with groans of sorrow.' He often used to say this to the Ministers and other friars, especially in General Chapter.

How he taught and wished that superiors and preachers should occupy themselves in prayer and in humble tasks.

FRANCIS, the faithful servant and perfect imitator of Christ, feeling himself wholly united to Christ through the virtue of holy humility, desired this humility in his friars before all other virtues. And in order that they might love, desire, acquire, and preserve it, he gave them constant encouragement by his own example and teaching, and particularly impressed this on the Ministers and preachers, urging them to undertake humble tasks.

He used to say that they must not allow the duties of high office or the responsibility of preaching to stand in the way of holy and devout prayer, going out for alms, doing manual labour when required, and carrying out other humble duties like the rest of the brethren, both as a good example and for the good of their own and others' souls. He said, 'The friars under obedience are much edified when their Ministers and preachers gladly devote their time to prayer, and apply themselves to humble and undistinguished tasks. Unless they do this they cannot admonish other friars without embarrassment, injustice, and self-condemnation; for if we follow Christ's example, we must act rather than teach, and our acting and teaching must go together.'

How he taught the friars to know when he was God's servant and when he was not.

BLESSED Francis once called together a large number of friars and said to them, 'I have asked God to show me when I am His servant and when I am not; for I have no wish to live except as His servant. And in His mercy the most gracious Lord has given me this answer: "You may know that you are My servant when your thoughts, words, and actions are holy." So I have called you together, my brothers, and disclosed this to you, so that whenever you see me lacking in all or any of these respects I may be put to shame in your eyes.'

75

How he particularly wanted all the friars to do manual labour from time to time.

HE used to say that brethren who were lacking in zeal and unwilling to apply themselves simply and humbly to any work would quickly be spewed out of God's mouth. No idler could appear before him without at once receiving a sharp rebuke, for he, who was the pattern of all perfection, worked humbly with his own hands, and never allowed God's best gift of time to be wasted.

He said, 'I wish all my brethren to work and to occupy themselves humbly in good works, so that we do not become a burden to other men, or allow our hearts and tongues to wander in idleness. So those who do not know a trade are to learn one.'

But he said that the profit and payment for work was not to be received by the workers but by the Guardians, who were to use it at their discretion for the good of the community.

PART IV

ON HIS ZEAL FOR THE OBSERVANCE OF THE RULE, AND FOR THE ORDER AS A WHOLE

76

Firstly, how he praised those who observed the Rule, and wished the friars to know the Rule, discuss it, and die in it.

BLESSED Francis, who observed the Holy Gospel perfectly and zealously, earnestly desired that all friars should observe the Rule, which itself is nothing other than a perfect observance of the Gospel; and he gave his especial blessing to those who are, and will be, zealous in this.

He used to tell his followers that our profession was the book of life, the hope of salvation, the pledge of glory, the heart of the Gospel, the way of the cross, the state of perfection, the key of paradise, and the compact of the eternal covenant. He wanted the Rule to be understood and accepted by all, and wished the friars to discuss it in their conferences, and meditate on it frequently by themselves, in order to remind them of their guiding vows. He also taught them that the Rule should be always before their eyes, as a reminder of the life they should lead and had bound themselves to follow. And, in addition, he wished and taught the friars that they should die with it before them.

77

On a holy lay-brother who was martyred holding the Rule in his hands.

ONE of the lay-brothers, whom we firmly believe to have been admitted into the choir of Martyrs, did not forget this sacred

D   95

ordinance and command of our blessed Father. For when he
went among the Saracens in his desire for martyrdom, and
while he was being led to martyrdom by the unbelievers, he
held the Rule in both hands with great fervour. And he knelt
down humbly before his companion and said, 'Dearest brother,
I confess myself guilty, before the eyes of the Divine Majesty
and before you, of all the offences that I have committed against
this Rule.'

After this short confession the sword fell and ended his life,
and he attained the crown of martyrdom. This man had entered
the Order so young that he could hardly bear the fasts imposed
by the Rule, but while still a boy he had worn a breastplate
next to his body. Happy young man, who began so happily,
and ended his life even more happily!

78

*How he wished the Order always to remain under the protection and
discipline of the Church.*

BLESSED Francis said, 'I will go and entrust the Order of Friars
Minor to the holy Roman Church. The rod of her authority
will daunt and restrain those who wish it ill, and the sons of
God will everywhere enjoy full freedom to pursue their eternal
salvation. Let her sons acknowledge the kindly blessings of their
Mother, and embrace her sacred feet with particular devotion.

'Under her protection no harm will come upon the Order, and
the son of Satan will not trample over the vineyard of the Lord
with impunity. Our holy Mother will herself imitate the glory
of our poverty, and will not permit our observance of humility
to be overshadowed by the cloud of pride. She will preserve
unimpaired the bonds of love and peace that exist between us,
and will impose her gravest censure on the unruly. The sacred
observance of evangelical poverty will ever flourish before her,

and she will never allow the fragrance of our good name and holy life to be destroyed.'

The four privileges granted by God to the Order and revealed to Saint Francis.

BLESSED Francis said that God had granted him four privileges, and made them known to him by an angel. These were: that the Order and profession of Friars Minor would endure until the Day of Judgement; that no one who deliberately persecuted the Order would live long; that no wrong-doers, who intended to live an evil life in the Order, would be able to remain in it for long; and that anyone who sincerely loved the Order, however great a sinner, would obtain mercy at the last.

On the qualities required in the Minister General and his colleagues.

So great was his zeal to maintain perfection in the Order, and so vital did he consider the perfect observance of the Rule, that he often wondered who might be suitable to govern the whole community after his death, and with God's help to maintain it in perfection; but he could not think of anyone.

Not long before his death, one of the friars said to him, 'Father, you will soon depart to God, and this family which has followed you will remain in this vale of tears. Give us some indication, therefore, if you know of any member of the Order in whom you have confidence, and on whom the burden of the Minister Generalship might worthily be laid.'

Breaking into frequent sighs as he spoke, blessed Francis replied, 'My son, I do not know of any leader suitable for so great and varied an army, or any shepherd for so vast and scattered a flock. But I will describe the qualities that the leader and shepherd of this family should possess. Such a man should be sober living, very discreet, of excellent reputation, and without personal attachments, so that he does not cause dissension in the Order by showing favour to individuals. He should be a lover of prayer, so that he will divide his time between the needs of his own soul and those of his flock. Early in the morning he should place the most holy Sacrifice of the Mass before all else, and spend much time at his devotions, lovingly commending himself and his flock to the protection of God. But when his prayer is ended, he should place himself at the disposal of the brethren and invite questions, answer their inquiries, and attend to the needs of all with charity, patience, and courtesy.

'He should not be *a respecter of persons*, and should devote as much attention to the simple and ignorant as to the wise and learned. Should he be granted the gift of learning, let him nevertheless show evidence of piety and simplicity, patience and humility in his behaviour. Let him foster these virtues in himself as well as in others, constantly exercising them in practice and inspiring others to do so by example rather than by words. He should loathe money, which is the chief corrupter of our profession and perfection. Being the head and example of the Order, he should be imitated by all, so let him never be engrossed in finances.

'His habit and breviary should be sufficient possessions for him; others can take care of his pen-case, quill, papers and seal. He should not collect books or be absorbed in much study, lest the time given to this detract from his proper duties. He should give devout comfort to those in trouble, for he is the ultimate resort of the distressed; for if they cannot obtain healing remedies from him, the disease of despair will overpower the afflicted. He should show mildness in order to bend the unruly to gentleness, and forego some of his own rights if it will win a soul. He should show pity to those who desert the Order, as to sheep who have perished, and never refuse mercy to them, realizing that temptations that could drive them to such a fall must have been overwhelming, and that were God to permit him to be tested in the same way, he might himself fall into an even deeper pit.

'I would have the Minister General, as Vicar of Christ, to be held in the greatest devotion and reverence by all, and his needs supplied with all goodwill in so far as our humble way of life allows. But he must not delight in honours, or be more pleased to receive favours than injuries; honours must not alter his way of life except for the better. Should he need better or more palatable food on occasion, he is not to take it in private but in public, so that others who are sick or frail may not be embarrassed when they need similar concessions.

'It is his particular duty to examine the secrets of the conscience, and to extract the truth from where it lies hidden. Let him at first regard all accusations as suspect, until truth begins to appear after careful inquiry. He should not pay attention to garrulous people, and when they accuse others he should treat them with particular reserve, and should not believe them too readily. He should be a man who would never betray or relax the proper forms of justice and equity in a desire to retain personal regard. He must at the same time take care that no soul is destroyed by excessive severity, that sloth is not aroused by undue lenience, or discipline undermined by careless indulgence. In this way he will be feared by all, and loved by those who fear him. But he should always remember and feel that his office of authority is a burden to him rather than an honour.

'I would like him to have as colleagues men of recognized honesty, who are firmly opposed to luxury, resolute in difficulty, kind and understanding to offenders, and having an equal affection for all. Men who take no reward for their work but their bare bodily needs, and who seek nothing but the glory of God, the welfare of the Order, the good of their own souls, and the well-being of all the brethren. Men who are agreeable to all whom they meet, and receive all who come to them with holy joy, demonstrating the ideal and observance of the Gospel and the Rule purely and simply in their own lives.

'This is the kind of man,' he said, 'who should be Minister-General of this Order, and these are the kind of colleagues that he ought to have.'

81

How God spoke to him when he was greatly distressed by friars who were falling away from perfection.

BECAUSE of the boundless zeal that he had at all times for the perfection of the Order, he was naturally distressed whenever he heard of or saw any imperfection in it. And beginning to realize that some of the friars were setting a bad example in the Order, and had begun to decline from the highest ideals of their profession, his heart was moved to the deepest grief, so that he once said to our Lord in prayer, 'Lord, I return to You the family which You have given me!' And at once the Lord answered him, 'Tell Me, O simple and ignorant little man, why are you so distressed when some brother deserts the Order, and when the friars do not follow the way that I have showed you? Tell Me, Who has founded this Order of friars? Who turns men to penitence? Who gives them grace to persevere in it? Is it not I? I have not chosen you to rule My family because you are a learned and eloquent man, for it is not My will that you or those who were true friars and true observants of the Rule should walk by the way of learning and eloquence. I have chosen you, a simple and unlearned man, so that both you and the others may realize that I will watch over My flock. And I have appointed you as a sign to them, in order that the things that I have performed in you may also be performed in them. For those who walk in the way that I have showed you possess Me, and shall possess Me even more fully; but those who walk by another way will be stripped of even what they seemed to possess. I tell you, therefore, do not be too distressed about the others, but continue to do as you are doing, and to work as you are working, for I have established the Order of friars in everlasting love. Rest assured that I have so great a love for the Order that if any brother returns to his own vomit and dies outside the Order, I will send another friar into the Order to win a crown in his place; and if such a friar has not been born, I will cause him to be born. And in order that you may know how sincerely I love the life and Order of the friars, I promise that were there only three friars remaining in the entire Order, it would still be My Order, and I will not abandon it to all eternity.'

And when he had heard these things, his soul was marvellously comforted.

And although, in his constant zeal for the perfection of the Order, he was not entirely able to restrain his vehement grief when he heard of any fault committed by the friars, through which a bad example or scandal might arise, after he had been comforted by the Lord in this way he called to mind the words of the psalm: *Never will I retract my oath to give Thy just commands observance.* He said, 'I have vowed to observe the Rule which the Lord Himself gave to me and to those who desire to follow me. And all these friars have vowed themselves to this as I have done. So now that I have laid down my responsibility for the brethren because of my infirmities and for other weighty reasons, I am not bound to do anything other than pray for the Order and show the friars a good example. For God has shown me, and I know it to be true, that if my infirmities did not excuse me, the greatest assistance that I could give to the Order would be to spend each day in prayer for it to God, Who governs, preserves, and maintains it. For I have bound myself before God and the brethren, that if any friar should perish through my bad example, I should be obliged to render account to God for him.'

These were the words that he used to repeat inwardly to

quieten his heart, and he often expounded them to the friars during addresses and Chapters. So if any friar ever told him that he ought to intervene in the government of the Order, he would reply, 'The friars already have their Rule, and they have vowed to observe it. And after God had been pleased to appoint me as their superior, I vowed before them that I would observe it myself, so that they would not be able to plead any excuse on my account. The friars already know what to do, and what to avoid, so that no duty remains for me except to set them an example by my own actions. This is why I have been given to them, both during my life and after my death.'

82

On the special devotion that he had for S. Mary of the Angels, and the rules that he made against idle conversation there.

As long as he lived he always had an especial zeal and desire to preserve the most perfect life and conversation in the holy house of S. Mary of the Angels above all other houses of the Order, because it was the head and mother of the entire Order. He intended and desired this place to be the very pattern and example of humility, poverty, and evangelical perfection to all other houses, and wished the friars living in it always to be more careful and thoughtful than others, both in avoiding evil and in doing everything which tends to the perfect observance of the Rule.

So in order to avoid idleness—which is the root of all evils, especially in a Religious—he once ordained that each day after their meal the friars should join him in some kind of work, so that they should not wholly or partly lose the benefit gained in time of prayer by useless and idle conversation, to which men are particularly prone after meals.

He also laid down and firmly ordered it to be observed, that if any friar walking with or working among the others uttered any idle remark, he was obliged to recite one *Our Father* and to say the *Praises of God* at the beginning and end of this prayer. Should he realize what he had done and confess his fault, he was to say the *Our Father* and *Praises* for his own soul. But if he were first rebuked by another friar, he was to say them for the soul of the friar who had corrected him. Similarly, if the guilty friar made excuses or refused to say the *Our Father*, he would be required to say it twice for the soul of the friar who had corrected him. But if, on his own evidence and that of another, it was established that he had gossiped, he was required in addition to say the *Praises* at the beginning and end of his prayer in a loud voice, so as to be heard and understood by all the friars near by; and while he was saying it, the other friars were to stand and listen. If any friar heard another passing idle remarks and kept silent without correcting him, he was required to say the *Our Father* and the *Praises* for the soul of the other friar. And any friar who entered a cell or house and found another of the brethren there was at once to praise and bless God devoutly.

The most holy Father was always careful to say these *Praises* himself, and taught them to the other friars with fervent will and desire; and he encouraged them to say the *Praises* reverently and devoutly.

83

How he told the friars never to leave S. Mary of the Angels.

ALTHOUGH blessed Francis was aware that the kingdom of heaven was established in every place on earth, and believed that the grace of God could everywhere be given to the faithful, he had learned from experience that S. Mary of the Angels was filled with richer grace and often visited by celestial spirits. So he often said to the friars, 'My sons, see that you never abandon this place! If you are driven out of one door, re-enter by another, for this place is holy indeed; it is the dwelling-place of Christ and His Virgin Mother. When we were few, it was here that the Most High increased us; it was here that He illumined the souls of His poor ones with the light of His wisdom; it was here that He kindled our desires with the fire of His love. Whosoever prays here with a devout heart shall obtain whatever he asks, while an evil-doer shall receive heavier punishment.

'My sons, regard this place as most worthy of all reverence and honour as the true dwelling-place of God, especially dear to Him and to His Mother. Glorify God the Father, and His Son Jesus Christ our Lord in the unity of the Holy Spirit in this place with all your hearts and with the voice of praise and confession.'

84

The favours granted by God in S. Mary of the Angels.

HOLY of Holies is this place of places,
Rightly deemed worthy of the highest honours!
Happy its surname 'of the holy Angels,'
Happier its dedication to 'Saint Mary':
And now the third name of 'The little Portion'
Foretells the Mother-House of all the Order.
Here the fair presence of the holy Angels
Sheds light around it, filling it with splendour;
Here in the long night-watches of the brethren
Praises soar upwards, piercing the heavens.
Once long abandoned, fallen into ruin,
Francis restored it to its former honour;
Of the three churches which the holy Father
Raised with his own hands, this is best and dearest.
This place our Father chose for his own dwelling,
Here in stern penance clad his limbs in sack-cloth,
Subdued his body and its errant passions,
Made it obedient to the spirit's bidding.
This holy temple God chose as the birthplace

Of the Friars Minor, humble, poor, and joyful,
While the example of the holy Father
Drew a great army, walking in his footsteps.
Here for the tonsure of her golden tresses
Came the sweet virgin Clare, the spouse of Jesus,
Casting behind her all the pomps and pleasures
Loved by the worldly, and embracing penance.
Here did the Orders of the Friars and Ladies
Spring into being, born of one fair Mother,
Mary most holy, who in her new offspring
Gave to the world new patterns of her First-born.
Here the broad highway of the old world changed
Into the narrow way to life eternal;
And to the faithful, called from every nation,
New grace was given freely by the Father.
Here was the Holy Rule to guide the Order
Written by Francis; Poverty exalted;
Pride was cast headlong, and the Cross upraised
Once more among us for the world's salvation.
Whenever Francis, worn and frail in body,
Weary in spirit, sought for rest and comfort,
In the sweet silence of this sanctuary
Here he found healing, comfort, and refreshment.
And when the Devil doubting and confusion
Sowed in his spirit, here was Truth revealed;
Here, too, was granted to the holy Father
All that he asked for in his intercession.

Part V

ON HIS ZEAL FOR THE PERFECTION OF THE FRIARS

85

Firstly, how he described the perfect friar.

THE most blessed Father, having in some degree transformed the friars into saints by the ardour of his love and by the fervent zeal for their perfection which fired him, often pondered on the virtues that ought to adorn a good Friar Minor. He used to say that a good Friar Minor should imitate the lives and possess the merits of these holy friars: the perfect faith and love of poverty of Brother Bernard; the simplicity and purity of Brother Leo, who was a man of most holy purity; the courtesy of Brother Angelo, who was the first nobleman to enter the Order, and was endowed with all courtesy and kindness; the gracious look and natural good sense of Brother Masseo, together with his noble and devout eloquence; the mind upraised to God, possessed in its highest perfection by Brother Giles; the virtuous and constant prayer of Brother Rufino, who prayed without ceasing, and whose mind was ever fixed on God, whether sleeping or working; the patience of Brother Juniper, who attained the state of perfect patience because he kept the truth of his low estate constantly in mind whose supreme desire was to follow Christ on the way of the Cross; the bodily and spiritual courage of Brother John of Lauds, who in his time had been physically stronger than all men; the charity of Brother Roger, whose whole life and conversation was inspired by fervent charity; the caution of Brother Lucidus, who was unwilling to remain in any place longer than a month, for when he began to like a place, he would at once leave it, saying, 'Our home is not here, but in heaven.'

Saint Francis tells the friars a parable about pure looks, in order to illustrate chaste conduct.

AFTER the fundamental virtue of holy humility, blessed Francis loved and wished to see pre-eminent in the friars among the other virtues that of fair and pure chastity. Wishing to teach the friars to have chaste eyes, he gave an example of impure looks by the following parable.

A devout and powerful king sent two messengers in succession to his queen. The first returned and simply reported the words of the queen, saying nothing about the queen herself. The other messenger returned, and having briefly delivered his message, gave a lengthy description of the queen's beauty. 'Indeed, Your Majesty,' he said, 'I have seen the most beautiful of women. Happy the man who enjoys her!'

The king said, 'Vile fellow, you have been casting impure looks on my queen! It is evident that you have secretly hoped to possess what you saw.' So he recalled the first messenger and said to him, 'What do you think of the queen?' 'She is an excellent lady,' he wisely replied, 'for she listened to me willingly and with patience.' Then the king asked, 'And do you think her beautiful?' He replied, 'Your Majesty, it is your privilege to look at her and decide this; my duty was only to deliver her message.' The king then made this decree, 'You have pure eyes; be chaste in body as well. You shall serve in my apartments and enjoy my pleasures. But this shameless fellow is to leave my palace lest he defile my bed.'

'Therefore,' said blessed Francis, 'who will not fear to gaze upon the bride of Christ?'

87

The three sayings that he left to the friars to preserve their perfection.

ONCE when he wanted to vomit because of his disease of the stomach, he did so with such violence that he brought up blood all night until morning. When his companions saw him almost dying from extreme exhaustion and pain, they said to him with the deepest grief and many tears, 'Father, what shall we do without you? To whose charge will you leave us orphans? You have always been father and mother to us; you have conceived and brought us forth in Christ. You have been our leader and shepherd, our instructor and corrector, teaching and correcting us by your example rather than by words. Where shall we go, sheep without a shepherd, children without a father, rough and simple men without a leader? Where shall we go to find you, O Glory of Poverty, Praise of Simplicity, and boast of our sinful nature? Who now will show us blind men the way of truth? How shall we hear your mouth speaking to us, and your tongue giving us counsel? Where will be your burning spirit, which guides us along the way of the Cross, and inspires us to evangelical perfection? Where will you be, so that we may run to you, light of our eyes? Where can we seek you, comfort of our souls? O Father, are you dying? You are leaving us abandoned, sad, and full of despair!

'Alas for this day! For a day of tears and bitterness, a day of desolation and grief is coming upon us! And no wonder, for your life has been a constant light to us, and your words have been like burning torches, always lighting us along the way of the Cross to evangelical perfection, and to the love and imitation of our sweet and crucified Lord.

'Father, at least give your blessing to us and to the other

108

friars, the sons whom you have begotten in Christ, and leave us some memorial of your will which the brethren can always have in remembrance, and say, "Our Father left these words to his friars and sons at his death." '

Then the most loving Father turned his eyes towards his sons, and said, 'Send Brother Benedict of Piratro to me.' For this friar was a holy and wise priest, who sometimes celebrated Mass for blessed Francis when he was lying ill; for however sick he might be, he always wished to hear Mass whenever possible. And when he had come, blessed Francis said, 'Write that I give my blessing to all my brethren in the Order, and to all who will enter it in time to come until the end of the world. And since I cannot speak much because of my weakness and the pain of my disease, I wish briefly to make my will and purpose clear to all the brethren, both present and to come. As a sign that they remember me, my blessing, and my Testament, I wish them always to love one another, as I have loved them. Let them always love and honour our Lady Poverty, and remain faithful and obedient to the bishops and clergy of holy Mother Church.'

At the close of Chapters, our Father always used to bless and absolve all the friars in the Order, both present and to come, and in the fervour of his love he often did so out of Chapter. But he used to warn the brethren that they must beware of setting a bad example, and he cursed all who by their bad example caused people to speak ill of the Order and life of the friars, since the good and holy friars are put to disgrace and great distress by such behaviour.

88

On the love that he showed the friars when nearing death, by giving to each a fragment of bread after the example of Christ.

ONE night blessed Francis was in such distress from the pain of his disease that he could not sleep or rest all night long. But at dawn, when his pain eased somewhat, he sent for all the friars in the house. And making them sit down before him, he looked upon them as representatives of the whole Order. And laying his right hand on the head of each in turn, he blessed them all, both present and absent, as well as those who were to enter the Order until the end of the world. And he seemed to grieve because he was unable to see all his friars and sons before his death.

But wishing to imitate his Lord and Master in his death as he had done so perfectly in his life, he ordered loaves to be brought to him. And having blessed them, he had them broken into many fragments, for his great weakness would not allow him to break them himself. Then he took the bread and gave a piece to each of the friars, asking them to eat all of it.

In this way, as on the Thursday before His death our Lord had desired to eat with His Apostles as a sign of His love, so did His perfect imitator blessed Francis wish to show the same sign of love to his own brethren. It is clear that he wished to do this in imitation of Christ, for he later inquired whether it were Thursday; and when he was told that it was another day, he said that he had thought it was Thursday.

One of the friars preserved a piece of this bread, and after the death of blessed Francis many sick people who tasted it were immediately healed of their diseases.

89

How he feared that the friars might be put to trouble by his illness.

WHILE he was unable to sleep because of his ailments, he realized that the friars were becoming very distracted and tired on his account. And because he had a deeper concern for their souls than for his own body, he began to fear that their constant efforts to serve him might cause them to commit some small offence against God through impatience.

So with great pity and compassion he once said to his companions, 'My dearest brothers and little sons, do not allow your labours for me in my illness be a burden to you, for God will repay you for me, His little servant; He will reward you with all the fruits of your labours, both in this world and the next. You will win more merit for the things that you have had to leave undone in your care for me in my illness, than if you had done them for yourselves; for whoever helps me helps the whole Order and life of the friars. In fact, you can say to me, "We are accumulating credit on your account, and God Himself will be in our debt." '

The holy Father spoke in these terms wishing to encourage and support their faint spirits, and moved by his great zeal for the perfection of their souls. For he was afraid that, because of their work for him, some of them might say, 'We cannot pray because we have so much work to do,' and becoming tired and impatient, they might lose the great reward due for their modest labours.

90

How he counselled the Sisters of Saint Clare.

AFTER blessed Francis had composed *The Praises of the Lord in His Creatures,* he also wrote some holy words with a melody to comfort and edify the Poor Ladies, knowing that they were in great distress over his illness. And being unable to visit them personally, he sent these words to them by his companions. For in these words he wished to make his purpose clear to them, namely, that they were to live and converse humbly, and be of one mind in charity. For he saw that their conversion and holy life was not only a source of glory to the Order of Friars, but of edification to the whole Church.

But knowing that from the beginning of their conversion they had led a life of great confinement and poverty, he always felt the greatest pity and compassion for them. So in these words he asked that as the Lord had gathered them together from many places into one in order to live in holy charity, poverty, and obedience, they must always persevere in them until death. He particularly emphasized that they should make proper provision for their bodily needs out of the alms that the Lord gave them with joy and thankfulness. And he asked above all that the healthy sisters be patient in their labours for the sick, and the sick be patient in their illnesses.

PART VI

ON HIS CONSTANT FERVOUR OF LOVE AND PITY
FOR THE PASSION OF CHRIST

91

Firstly, how he had no thought for his own infirmities because of his devotion to the Passion of Christ.

So fervent were the love and compassion of blessed Francis for the sorrows and sufferings of Christ, and so deep was his inward and outward grief over the Passion day by day that he had never considered his own infirmities. Consequently, although he suffered from ailments of the stomach, spleen, and liver over a long period until the day of his death, and had endured constant pain in his eyes ever since his return from overseas, he was never willing to undergo any treatment for its cure.

So the Lord Cardinal of Ostia, seeing how harsh he had always been on his own body, and how he was already beginning to lose his sight because he refused to undergo a cure, urged him with great kindness and compassion, saying, 'Brother, you are not doing right in refusing treatment, for your life and health are of great value not only to the friars, but to the layfolk and the whole Church. You have always had a great sympathy for your brethren when they are sick, and have always been kindly and merciful; you must not be cruel to yourself in so great a need. I therefore order you to have yourself cured and helped.' For because the most holy Father took boundless delight in imitating the humility and example of the Son of God, he always regarded anything unpleasant to the body as welcome.

How he was found loudly lamenting the Passion of Christ as he walked along.

A SHORT while after his conversion, as he was walking alone along the road not far from the church of S. Mary of the Porziuncula, he was uttering loud cries and lamentations as he went. And a spiritually-minded man who met him, fearing that he was suffering from some painful ailment, said to him, 'What is your trouble, brother?' But he replied, 'I am not ashamed to travel through the whole world in this way, bewailing the Passion of my Lord.' At this, the man joined him in his grief, and began to weep aloud.

We have known this man and learned of this incident through him. He is one who has shown great kindness and compassion to blessed Francis and to us who were his companions.

How his outward signs of joy sometimes gave place to tears and compassion for Christ.

INTOXICATED by love and compassion for Christ, blessed Francis sometimes used to act in ways like these. For the sweetest of spiritual melodies would often well up within him and found expression in French melodies, and the murmurs of God's voice, heard by him alone, would joyfully pour forth in the French tongue.

Sometimes he would pick up a stick from the ground, and laying it on his left arm, he would draw another stick across it with his right hand like a bow, as though he were playing a viol or some other instrument; and he would imitate the movements of a musician and sing in French of our Lord Jesus Christ.

But all this jollity would end in tears, and his joy would melt away in compassion for the sufferings of Christ. And at such times he would break into constant sighs, and in his grief would forget what he was holding in his hands, and be caught up in spirit into heaven.

PART VII

ON HIS ZEAL FOR PRAYER AND THE DIVINE OFFICE, AND HIS DESIRE TO PRESERVE THE SPIRIT OF JOY IN HIMSELF AND IN OTHERS

94

Firstly, on prayer and the Divine Office.

ALTHOUGH he had been troubled for many years by the infirmities already described, he was so devout and reverent at prayer and the Divine Office that whenever he was at prayer or reciting the Divine Office he would never lean against a wall or support. He always stood upright and bareheaded, although he sometimes knelt. Indeed, he devoted the greater part of the day and night to prayer, and even when he was travelling around on foot, he would always halt when he wished to say the Hours. But if he were riding because of his infirmity, he would always dismount to say the Office.

One day it was raining heavily, and he was riding because of his infirmity and pressing need. And although he was already drenched to the skin, he dismounted from the horse when he wished to say the Hours, and said the Office standing in the road with the rain pouring down on him, as though he had been in a church or cell. And he said to his companion, 'If the body likes to take its food in peace and at ease, although it becomes food for worms, how much greater should be the soul's reverence and devotion when it receives the food which is God Himself.'

How he always loved spiritual joy, both in himself and others.

IT was always the supreme and particular desire of blessed Francis to possess an abiding joy of spirit outside times of prayer and Divine Office. This was the virtue that he especially loved to see in his brethren, and he often reproached them when they showed signs of gloom and despondency.

He used to say, 'If the servant of God strives to obtain and preserve both outwardly and inwardly the joyful spirit which springs from purity of heart and is acquired through devout prayer, the devils have no power to hurt him, and say, "We can find no way to get at him or hurt him, because this servant of God preserves his joy both in trouble and in prosperity." But the devils are delighted when they discover means to quench or disturb the devotion and joy which springs from true prayer and other holy practices. For if the devil can obtain a hold over one of God's servants, he will soon transform a single hair into a log to hurl at him unless he is a wise man and takes care to remove and destroy it as quickly as possible by the power of holy prayer, contrition, and satisfaction.

'Therefore, my brothers, since this spiritual joy springs from cleanness of heart and the purity of constant prayer, it must be your first concern to acquire and preserve these two virtues, so as to possess this inward joy that I so greatly desire and love to see both in you and myself, and which edify our neighbour and reproach our enemy. For it is the lot of the Devil and his minions to be sorrowful, but ours always to be happy and rejoice in the Lord.'

How he censured one of his companions for showing a gloomy face.

BLESSED Francis used to say, 'Although I know that the devils envy me the blessings that God has given me, I also know and see that they cannot harm me through myself, so they plan and try to hurt me through my companions. But if they cannot hurt me either through myself or through my companions, they retire in great confusion. Indeed, whenever I am tempted or depressed, if I see my companions joyful, I immediately turn away from my temptation and oppression, and regain my own inward and outward joy.'

So the Father used to censure those who went about with gloomy faces, and once rebuked a friar who appeared with a gloomy face, saying, 'Why are you making an outward display of grief and sorrow for your sin? This sorrow is between God and yourself alone. So pray Him in His mercy to pardon you and restore to your soul the joy of His salvation, of which the guilt of your sins has deprived it. Always do your best to be cheerful when you are with me and the other brethren; it is not right for a servant of God to show a sad and gloomy face to his brother or to anyone else.'

It should not be imagined, however, that our Father, who loved dignified and sensible behaviour, wished this spiritual joy to be shown in levity or empty chatter, for these things are not evidence of spiritual joy, but of emptiness and folly. He greatly disliked laughter and idle gossip in a servant of God; in fact, he preferred him not to laugh, and to avoid giving others any occasion for hilarity. In one of his Counsels he gave an even clearer definition of the nature of spiritual joy in a servant of God, saying, 'Blessed is the Religious who has no pleasure or joy except in the most holy sayings and works of the Lord, and by these inspires men to the love of God in joy and gladness.

And woe to the Religious who takes delight in idle and foolish talk, and by them provokes men to laughter.'

By a joyful face, therefore, he understood fervour, thoughtfulness, and the disposition and preparation of mind and body to a ready undertaking of every good work; for this fervour and readiness often have a greater influence on people than by the good deed itself. Indeed, however good an action may be, if it does not seem to have been done willingly and fervently, it tends to produce distaste rather than edification. So he did not wish to see a gloomy face, which often betrays a sluggish body and a melancholy mind. He always loved to see gravity of face and deportment both in himself and others, and did his best to encourage this by word and example. For experience had taught him that grave and restrained behaviour provided a wall and strong shield against the darts of the devils; he knew that without the protection of this wall and shield the soul resembled an unarmed soldier among powerful and well-armed enemies, ever eager and intent on his death.

97

How he told the friars to satisfy their bodily needs, lest prayer be lost through sickness.

OUR most holy Father, knowing that the body was created to serve the soul, and that bodily actions were to be performed for spiritual ends, used to say, 'In eating, sleeping, and satisfying the other needs of the body, the servant of God should make sensible provision for his Brother Body so that he may not have cause to complain and say, "I cannot stand upright and continue at prayer, nor can I be cheerful in my troubles or do other good things, because you do not provide for my needs." But if the servant of God satisfies his body wisely, adequately, and suitably, and Brother Body wants to be careless, fat, and sleepy in prayer, vigils, and other

119

good works, then he must punish him like a fat and idle beast of burden, because he wants to eat but not to be useful and carry his load. However, if Brother Body cannot have what he needs in health or sickness because of want and poverty, and has humbly and honestly asked it of his brother or superior for the love of God, but has not received it, let him bear it patiently for love of our Lord, Who will comfort him; for Christ Himself endured want, and found no comfort. And if he bears this want patiently, God will credit it to him as his martyrdom. And because he has done whatsoever he could—and humbly asked for his needs—he will be absolved from all blame, even though his body become gravely ill as a result.'

PART VIII

ON CERTAIN TEMPTATIONS WHICH THE LORD
ALLOWED TO ASSAIL HIM

98

Firstly, how the devil entered a pillow under his head.

WHILE blessed Francis was staying in the hermitage of Greccio he was at prayer one night in the last cell beyond the large cell, and during the early hours of the night he called to his companion who was sleeping near him. This friar rose and came to the door of blessed Francis's cell, and the saint said to him, 'Brother, I have not been able to sleep to-night, and I can't stand up to pray because my head shakes and my knees tremble violently. I think I must have eaten some darnel bread.'

When the friar had expressed his sympathy, blessed Francis said, 'I am sure that the devil is in this pillow under my head!' (For ever since he had left the world he had always declined to lie on a feather mattress or use a feather pillow, but the friars had compelled him against his will to have this pillow because of his disease of the eyes.) So he threw it to his companion, who caught it in his right hand and laid it on his left shoulder. But directly he passed through the door of the cell, he lost his speech, and could neither put down the pillow nor move his arms. So he stood there upright, with his senses benumbed and unable to stir from the spot. Having stood like this for some while, by the grace of God blessed Francis called to him; and at once he regained his senses, and let the pillow fall behind his back.

Coming back to blessed Francis, he told him what had happened to him, and the saint said, 'While I was saying Compline late last evening I felt the devil entering the cell. And I know that the devil is very cunning, for when he realized that he could not harm my soul, he wanted to prevent my body receiving its needs, so that I could neither sleep nor stand up to pray. He thought that he would disturb my devotion and joy of heart in this way, and make me complain of my affliction.'

99

On the grave temptation that he endured for more than two years.

WHILE he was living in the friary of S. Mary, a very grave temptation was inflicted on him for the good of his soul. He was so tormented in mind and body by this, that he often withdrew from the company of the friars because he could not show them his usual cheerfulness. Nevertheless, he continued to discipline himself by abstinence from food, drink, and speech; and he prayed more constantly and shed more abundant tears, so that the Lord might be pleased to grant some remedy strong enough for so great a trial.

When he had been troubled in this way for more than two years, he happened to be praying in the church of S. Mary one day, when he heard in spirit the words of the Gospel: *If you have faith, though it be but like a grain of mustard seed, you have only to say to this mountain, Remove from this place to that, and it will remove.* At once blessed Francis asked, 'Lord, what is this mountain?' And the reply came, 'This mountain is your temptation.' 'In that case, Lord,' said blessed Francis, 'let it happen with me as You have said.' And from that moment he was so completely freed that it seemed to him as though he had never had any temptation.

In the same way, at the time when he received the Stigmata of our Lord in his own body on the holy mountain of La Verna,

122

he suffered so many temptations and troubles from the devils that he could not display his former joy. And he told his companion (*Brother Leo*), 'If the brethren knew how many great trials and afflictions the devils bring upon me, there is not one of them who would not be moved to compassion and pity for me.'

100

How he was plagued by mice; and how the Lord comforted him, and assured him of His Kingdom.

TWO years before his death, while he was staying at S. Damian in a cell made of rush-mats, he was suffering intensely from his disease of the eyes, and for more than fifty days he could not bear the light of day, or even firelight. And in order to increase both his affliction and his merit, God allowed a horde of mice to infest the walls of his cell, and they ran over and around him day and night, so that he could neither pray nor rest. Even when he was eating, they climbed onto his table and worried him greatly, so that both he and his companions clearly recognized it as a temptation by the devil.

So one night, tormented by so many troubles and feeling sorry for himself, he prayed inwardly, 'Lord, look on me and help me in my troubles, and give me strength to bear them patiently.' And at once he heard a voice within his soul, saying, 'Tell Me, brother; if in recompense for these infirmities and tribulations you were to be given so vast and precious a treasure that, were the whole world pure gold, its stones jewels, and all its waters balsam, you would regard them as nothing in comparison to this vast treasure, would not you be very happy?' And blessed Francis replied, 'Lord, such a treasure would be vast and precious, very lovely and desirable.' And he heard the voice speaking to him once more, 'Then be glad, brother, and rejoice in your troubles and infirmities. As for the rest, trust in Me, as though you were already in My Kingdom.'

123

Rising early, he said to his companions, 'If an Emperor were to grant a whole kingdom to one of His slaves, ought not that slave to be full of joy? And if he were to bestow his entire empire on that slave, would be not be even happier?' And he continued, 'I should therefore rejoice in my infirmities and troubles, and *be strong in the Lord*, always giving thanks to God the Father, and to His only Son Jesus Christ, and to the Holy Spirit, for the great grace granted me by the Lord, for He has deigned to assure me, His unworthy servant, of His Kingdom while still living in the flesh. So, to His praise, for our own comfort and to edify our neighbours, I want to compose a new *Praise of the Lord in His creatures*; for we daily make use of them, and cannot live without them, and through them the human race greatly offends their Creator. For we are always ungrateful for His many graces and blessings, and do not praise the Lord, the Creator and Giver of all good gifts, as we should.' And sitting down, he began to meditate awhile.

Afterwards he said, *Most High, Almighty, good Lord, etc.*, and he set the words to a melody, and taught his companions to recite and sing it. For his soul was so full of consolation and sweetness at that time that he wished to send for Brother Pacificus, who had been known in the world as 'The King of Verse' and had been master of the choir at a noble court, and he wanted to give him a number of good and spiritual friars, who could go around the world with him, reciting and singing the *Praises of the Lord*. He said that he would like the friar who was the best preacher to speak to the people first, and afterwards they were all to sing the *Praises of the Lord* together as minstrels of God. And when the *Praises* were ended, the preacher was to say to the people, 'We are God's minstrels, and ask you to repay us for our songs by living in true penitence.' 'For what are God's servants but His minstrels,' he said, 'who must inspire the hearts of men and stir them to spiritual joy.' And in so saying, he referred particularly to the Friars Minor, whom God had given to the people for their salvation.

PART IX

ON THE SPIRIT OF PROPHECY

101

Firstly, how he foretold the restoration of peace between the Bishop and Mayor of Assisi through the influence of the Praises of the Creatures which he had composed and ordered his companions to sing before them.

AFTER blessed Francis had composed *The Praises of the Creatures*, which he called *The Song of Brother Sun*, a serious dispute happened to arise between the Bishop of Assisi and the Mayor. As a result, the Bishop excommunicated the Mayor, and the Mayor issued an order forbidding anyone to sell anything to the Bishop, to buy anything from him, or to make any agreement with him.

Although blessed Francis was ill when he heard of this, he was deeply grieved on their account, especially as there was no one to make peace between them. And he said to his companions, 'It brings great disgrace on us when the Bishop and Mayor hate one another in this way, and no one can make peace between them.' So he immediately wrote a verse to be included in the *Praises* for this occasion, and said:

> *Praise to Thee, my Lord, for those who pardon one another*
> *For love of Thee, and endure*
> *Sickness and tribulation;*
>
> *Blessed are they who shall endure it in peace,*
> *For they shall be crowned by Thee,*
> *O Most High.*

Then he called one of his companions and said, 'Go to the Mayor, and ask him from me to go to the Bishop's house with the city councillors and any others he can bring with him.' And when this friar had left, he said to two other companions, 'Go and sing *The Song of Brother Sun* before the Bishop, the Mayor, and those who are with them. I trust that the Lord will at once humble their hearts, and that they will return to their former affection and friendship.'

So when the whole company had assembled in the cloister-garth of the Bishop's house, the two friars rose, and one of them said, 'Blessed Francis in his sickness has composed a *Praise of the Lord in His Creatures*, in order to praise the Lord and edify his fellow men, so he asks you to listen to it with great devotion.' And they began to recite and sing it.

At once the Mayor rose and clasped his hands, listening with the greatest devotion, as though he were hearing the Lord's Gospel; and he wept profusely, for he had great faith in blessed Francis and a great devotion to him. And when the *Praises of the Lord* were ended, the Mayor said before the whole company, 'I solemnly assure you that I forgive the Lord Bishop, and wish to acknowledge him as my lord. And even if some man had slain my brother or my son, I would forgive him.' With these words, he cast himself at the Bishop's feet, and said to him, 'See now, for the love of our Lord Jesus Christ and of His servant blessed Francis I am willing to offer any amends that you please.' But the Bishop took him by the hands and raised him, saying, 'My office requires me to be humble, but I am quick-tempered by nature; I therefore beg you to forgive me.' So they embraced and kissed one another with great kindness and affection.

The friars were astonished and overjoyed when they saw that the reconciliation which blessed Francis had foretold had been thus fulfilled to the letter. And all present regarded it as a great miracle, and attributed it wholly to the merits of blessed Francis, that the Lord had moved them so swiftly, and that without uttering a word they had turned back from great discord and scandal to complete harmony.

But we who were with blessed Francis testify that whenever he said of anything, 'This is so,' or 'This will be,' it always took place to the letter. And we have seen this happen so often that it would take us a long time to write or describe it.

102

How he foretold the fall of a friar who refused to confess under the pretext of observing silence.

THERE was once a friar who was outwardly a man of sincere and holy life, and seemed to pray constantly day and night. And he observed perpetual silence, so that whenever he confessed to a priest, he did so by signs instead of words. He seemed so devout and fervent in the love of God that when he sometimes sat with the other brethren, although he did not speak, he was filled with inward and outward joy at hearing devout conversation, and thus moved other friars to devotion.

But when he had followed this way of life for several years, blessed Francis happened to visit the place where he was living. And learning of his way of life from the other friars, he told them, 'It is most certainly a temptation of the devil that makes him unwilling to confess.' Meanwhile the Minister General came to visit blessed Francis, and began to praise this friar to him. But blessed Francis said, 'Believe me, Brother, this friar has been led away and deceived by a wicked spirit.' The Minister General replied, 'It seems strange and almost incredible to me that this could be the case when the man shows so many signs of holiness and good works.' But blessed Francis said, 'Test him by telling him to confess at least once or twice a week in Chapter. If he refuses to obey, you will know that what I have said is true.'

So the Minister General said to the friar, 'Brother, I require

E 127

you to confess twice, or at least once, in Chapter.' But the friar laid his finger on his lips, shaking his head and showing by signs that he was not willing to do so because of his love for silence. And fearing to offend him, the Minister let him go. But not many days later this friar left the Order of his own will, and returned to the world wearing secular clothes.

One day two companions of blessed Francis chanced to be walking along a certain road when they met this man, who was walking alone like a very poor pilgrim. Feeling sorry for him, they said, 'Wretched man, what has happened to your sincere and holy way of life? For once you refused to speak or explain yourself to your brethren, and now you go wandering about the world like a man who knows nothing of God!' And he began to talk to them, often swearing 'By my faith!', which is a common worldly expression. And they said, 'Unhappy man! Why do you swear by your faith like worldly men? Once you used to keep silence, not only from idle words, but even from good words.' So they parted company, and not long afterwards he died. And we were all amazed when we realized how everything that blessed Francis had foretold when the friars had regarded the man as a saint had come true to the letter.

103

On the man who begged Saint Francis with tears to admit him into the Order.

AT the time when no one was admitted into the Order without the approval of blessed Francis, the son of a nobleman of Lucca came with many others who wished to enter the Order to see blessed Francis, who was then lying ill in the palace of the Bishop of Assisi. And when they all presented themselves to blessed Francis, he bowed before him and began to weep aloud, begging him to admit him. But blessed Francis looked at him and said, 'Wretched and worldly man, why are you lying to the Holy Spirit and to me? Your tears are worldly and not spiritual.'

And while he was speaking, the man's relatives arrived outside
the palace on horseback, wishing to seize him and carry him
back with them. Hearing the clatter of horses, he looked through
a window and saw his relatives. And at once he went down to
them, and returned to the world with them as blessed Francis
had foreseen.

104

On the priest's vineyard, which was stripped of its grapes because of
Saint Francis.

BLESSED Francis was once staying with a poor priest at the
church of S. Fabian near Rieti because of his disease of the eyes,
and the Lord Pope Honorius was visiting the city with his whole
court at the same time. And because of their devotion to blessed
Francis, many cardinals and other high clergy came to see him
almost daily.

Now this church had a small vineyard adjoining the house
where blessed Francis was lodged, and nearly all those who
visited him passed through the vineyard to the door of the
house. And because the grapes were ripe and the place very
pleasant, the entire vineyard was stripped and despoiled of its
grapes. So the priest began to feel indignant, saying, 'Although
it is a small vineyard, I used to make sufficient wine from it for
my needs, but this year I have lost the whole crop.'

When blessed Francis heard of this he sent for him, and said,
'Father, do not worry any more, for we cannot do anything
about it now. But trust in the Lord, for He is able to repair your
loss in full for the sake of me, His little servant. Tell me, how
many measures of wine did you obtain when your vineyard
was at its best?' 'Thirteen measures, Father,' the priest replied.
Blessed Francis said to him, 'Have no more regrets, and say no
hard words because of this. Trust in God and my word, and if
you obtain less than twenty measures of wine, I will have it

129

made up to you.' So the priest kept silence and said no more; and at the time of vintage he obtained no less than twenty measures of wine. And the priest was amazed, as were all who heard of it, and said that even if the vineyard had been full of grapes, it could not have produced twenty measures of wine.

But we who were with him testify that what he said about this, and everything else that he foretold, was always fulfilled to the letter.

105

How the knights of Perugia obstructed his preaching.

WHILE blessed Francis was preaching in the square at Perugia, some knights of Perugia began to canter around the square on horseback, exercising with their weapons. This greatly hindered his preaching, and although those who were listening protested, they refused to desist. So blessed Francis turned to them, and said in great fervour of spirit: 'Listen, and understand what the Lord proclaims through me, His little servant; and don't say, "This is a fellow from Assisi!"' (He said this because there was, and still is, a long-standing feud between the men of Perugia and Assisi.) And he went on, 'God has elevated you above your neighbours, and because of this you should be all the more ready to acknowledge your Creator by being humble, both towards God and to your neighbours. But your hearts are swollen with pride, and you attack your neighbours and kill many of them. I warn you that unless you speedily turn to God and compensate those whom you have injured, God Who leaves no crime unpunished will cause you to rise up against one another to your greater hurt and disgrace. You will be rent asunder by sedition and civil strife, and suffer far greater damage than your neighbours could ever inflict on you.'

For blessed Francis would never remain silent when he preached on the sins of the people, but rebuked them all openly and boldly. But the Lord had endowed him with such grace that all who heard and saw him, whatever their rank and condition, felt a great fear and reverence for him because he possessed the grace of God in such abundance. So men were always edified by his words, however severely they were rebuked by him, and were either converted to God or pricked in conscience.

A few days later God permitted a dispute to arise between the knights and the citizens, as a result of which the people drove the knights out of the city. And the knights, supported by the Church, devastated their fields, vineyards, and trees, and wrought every possible evil on the people. In retaliation, the people wrecked all the property of the knights, and both people and knights were punished just as blessed Francis had foretold.

106

How he foresaw the secret temptation and trouble of one of the friars.

ONE of the friars, a sincerely spiritual man and a friend of blessed Francis, had for many days been subjected to very severe temptations by the devil, and was almost reduced to despair. Every day he was so tormented by temptation that he was ashamed to confess as often as he should, and because of this he afflicted himself with much fasting, vigils, tears, and scourging.

By the will of God blessed Francis came to this friary, and one day while this brother was walking with him, the Father was enlightened by the Holy Spirit as to his trouble and temptation. Withdrawing a short distance from the friar who was walking with him, he turned to the troubled brother and said, 'Dearest Brother, henceforward I do not wish you to feel obliged to confess these temptations of the devil. And do not be afraid, for they have not harmed your soul. But, with my approval, say seven *Our Fathers* whenever they trouble you.'

The friar was very relieved when blessed Francis told him

that he was not obliged to confess them, for he had been very uneasy in mind on this matter. But he was dumbfounded that blessed Francis knew about this thing, which was known only to the priests to whom he had made his confession. And by the grace of God and the merits of blessed Francis he was immediately delivered from his temptation, and thenceforward continued in the greatest peace and tranquillity. And it was because the Saint had hoped for this that he confidently excused him from confession.

107

On the things that he foretold of Brother Bernard, and how they were all fulfilled.

NOT long before his death, some tasty food was prepared for blessed Francis, whereupon he thought of Brother Bernard, who was the first friar that he had. Saying to his companions, 'This dish is good for Brother Bernard,' he immediately sent for him. When Brother Bernard arrived, he sat down beside the bed where the Saint was lying, and said to him, 'Father, I beg you to bless me and give me some sign of affection, for if you show your paternal love towards me, I am sure that God Himself and the brethren will love me more.'

Blessed Francis could not see him, because he had already lost the sight of his eyes many days before; but he reached out his right hand and laid it on the head of Brother Giles, the third of the friars, thinking that he was laying it on the head of Brother Bernard, who was sitting beside him. Immediately aware of this through the Holy Spirit, he said, 'This is not the head of my Brother Bernard.' Then Brother Bernard came closer, and laying his hand on his head, blessed Francis gave him his blessing. Then he said to one of his companions, 'Write down what I tell you. Brother Bernard was the first friar that the Lord gave me, and he was first to observe the absolute perfection of the

Gospel by giving all his property to the poor. Because of this, and because of his many other merits, I cannot help loving him more than any other friar in the whole Order. As far as I may, I therefore desire and decree that whoever becomes Minister General is to love and honour him as they would myself. Let the Minister and all the friars of the Order regard him as taking my place.' And Brother Bernard and the other friars were greatly comforted by his words.

Knowing the sublime perfection of Brother Bernard, blessed Francis had prophesied before a number of friars, saying, 'Some of the most powerful and cunning devils have been assigned to tempt Brother Bernard, and they will bring many troubles and trials upon him. But as his end is drawing near the Lord in His mercy will take away all his troubles and temptations, and will establish such peace and consolation in his soul that all the brethren who see it will be filled with wonder, and reverence it as a great miracle. And in this peace and consolation of soul and body he will pass away to the Lord.'

To the great wonder of all the friars who heard these things from blessed Francis all his words about Brother Bernard were fulfilled to the letter. For during the illness that led to his death Brother Bernard enjoyed such peace and consolation of spirit that he did not want to lie down. And whenever he did so, he reclined in a sitting position so that no faintness, however slight, might mount to his head and interrupt his contemplation of God, or bring about sleep or delirium. And whenever he felt this happening, he would at once start up and strike himself, saying, 'What was that? Why was I thinking of that?' And he refused to accept any medicine, but said to the friar who offered it, 'Do not disturb me.'

In order to die in greater freedom and peace, Brother Bernard thenceforward entrusted the care of his body to one of the brethren who was a doctor, saying, 'I do not wish to be consulted about what I eat or drink. I leave that to you. If you give it me, I will take it; if you do not, I shall not ask for it.' But when he began to grow weaker he wished to have a priest always with him until the hour of his death; and whenever he remembered anything that burdened his conscience, he confessed it forthwith. After death his flesh became white and soft, and he seemed to smile, so that he became more lovely in his death than in his life. And all were even happier to gaze at him dead than alive, for he seemed 'a smiling saint' indeed.

108

How, shortly before his death, Saint Francis promised blessed Clare that she should see him; and how this came about after his death.

DURING the week in which blessed Francis died, Lady Clare, the first flower of the Poor Sisters of S. Damian in Assisi, feared that she might die before him, for they were both seriously ill at that time. She wept bitterly and could not be comforted, because she thought that she would be unable to see blessed Francis, her only Father after God, before her death, for he had been her comforter and teacher, and had first established her in the grace of God.

So she sent word of her fears by one of the friars, and when he heard of it, the Saint was moved with compassion for her, for he loved her with an especial and paternal affection. But realizing that he could not fulfil her desire to see him, he wrote a letter to comfort her and all the Sisters, and sent her his blessing. And he absolved her from any fault that she might have committed against his counsel and against the commands and teachings of the Son of God. And so that she might put aside all sadness, he was guided by the Holy Spirit to say to the friar whom she had sent, 'Go and tell the Lady Clare to put aside all sorrow and grief, for she cannot see me now. But promise her that before her death both she and her Sisters shall certainly see me, and be greatly comforted because of me.'

Soon afterwards, when blessed Francis had passed away in the night, all the people and clergy of Assisi came very early to take his holy body from the place where he had died, and they all sang hymns and praises and carried branches of trees. And by the will of God they bore him to S. Damian, so that the words that God had spoken through blessed Francis to comfort his daughters should be fulfilled.

And when the iron grille through which the Sisters used to receive Communion and hear the word of God had been removed, the friars lifted the holy body from its bier and raised it in their arms in front of the window for a long while. And Lady Clare and her sisters were comforted by this, although they were filled with grief and wept aloud when they saw themselves deprived of the consolation and counsel of so great a Father.

109

How he foretold that his body would be honoured after his death.

ONE day, while blessed Francis was lying ill in the house of the Bishop of Assisi, a spiritual friar said to him with a smile, as though joking, 'How much would you charge the Lord Bishop for all your sackcloth? One day many canopies and silken palls will cover this little body of yours which is now clothed in sackcloth!' For at that time he had a cowl patched with sacking, and a habit of sacking.

And blessed Francis—speaking not with his own words but with those of the Holy Spirit—replied with great fervour and joy of soul, 'What you say is true, for it will be to the praise and glory of my Lord!'

PART X

ON GOD'S PROVIDENCE FOR HIM IN MATERIAL THINGS

110

Firstly, how the Lord provided for the friars who were sharing their frugal meal with a doctor.

ONE day, while blessed Francis was staying in the hermitage of Fonte Colombo near Rieti because of his disease of the eyes, the oculist visited him. When he had stayed some while and was about to take his leave, blessed Francis said to one of his companions, 'Go and give the doctor the best meal that you can.' The friar replied, 'Father, I am ashamed to say that we are so poor at the moment that it would embarrass us to invite him to a meal.' Blessed Francis replied, 'O man of little faith, don't make me repeat my order!' Then the doctor said to blessed Francis, 'Brother, it is because the friars are so poor that it would give me all the more pleasure to eat with them.' For the doctor was a very rich man, and although blessed Francis and his companions had often invited him to a meal, he had not hitherto accepted.

So the brethren went and laid the table, and with great embarrassment they placed on it a little bread and wine, together with a few cabbages that they had prepared for themselves. When they had sat down to their frugal meal and begun to eat, there was a knock at the door of the house. One of the friars rose and opened it, and there stood a woman carrying a large hamper full of fine bread, fish, crayfish patties, honey and fresh grapes, which had been sent to blessed Francis by the lady of a castle about seven miles away.

The friars and the doctor were amazed and delighted when they saw this, and recalling the holiness of blessed Francis, they ascribed it wholly to his merits. Then the doctor said to the friars, 'My brothers, neither you nor we realize the great holiness of this man!'

111

On the fish that he craved during his illness.

ON another occasion, when blessed Francis was very ill in the palace of the Bishop of Assisi, the friars begged him to take some nourishment. 'I have no inclination to eat,' he replied, 'but if I could have a little angel-fish I might be able to eat it.'

No sooner had he spoken than a man came in carrying a basket containing three large and well-cooked angel-fish, together with some crayfish delicacies which had been sent him by Brother Gerard, the Minister at Rieti. And the holy Father ate these with pleasure. The friars were amazed at God's providence, and praised the Lord Who had provided these things for His servant, for such food was unobtainable in Assisi during the winter.

112

On the food and cloth that he wanted at his death.

ONE day at S. Mary of the Angels, during blessed Francis's last illness which was to cause his death, he called his companions together and said, 'You know how the Lady Jacoba of Settesoli has been and is most faithful and devoted to our Order and to me. I am sure that she will regard it as a great favour and consolation if you inform her of my condition. Ask her especially to send me some plain ashen-coloured cloth, and with it some of that sweetmeat that she has often made for me in the City.' (This is the sweetmeat which the people of Rome call *mostaccioli*, and is made of almonds, sugar, and other ingredients.) For the Lady Jacoba was a sincerely spiritual woman, and belonged to one of the noblest and richest families in the whole of Rome. Through the merits and preaching of blessed Francis she had received such grace from God that she seemed like another Magdalene, full of tears and devotion for the love and sweetness of Christ.

So the brethren wrote a letter as the Saint had instructed them, and one of the friars went to find a brother to take the letter to the lady. But suddenly there was a knock at the friary gate, and when one of the friars opened it, there stood the Lady Jacoba, who had come in great haste to visit blessed Francis. Directly he knew this, one of the friars hastened to blessed Francis and told him with much joy how the Lady Jacoba had arrived from Rome with her son and many other people to visit him. 'What shall we do, Father?' he inquired. 'Shall we allow her to enter and come to you?' (He asked this because in order to preserve good order and devotion at S. Mary's, blessed Francis had made a rule that no woman should enter the enclosure.) Blessed Francis replied, 'This rule need not be observed in the case of Lady Jacoba, whose faith and devotion have impelled her to travel here from such a distance.'

So Lady Jacoba came in to blessed Francis, and when she saw him, she wept. Wonderful to relate, she had brought ashen-coloured cloth for a habit, and everything mentioned in the letter as though she had already received it. And she told the friars, 'My brothers, while I was at prayer I was told in spirit, "Go and visit your Father, blessed Francis. Hurry, and do not delay, for you will not find him alive if you wait long. And take with you this cloth for a habit, and such and such things, and make him some of that sweetmeat. Take with you also a large amount of wax for candles, and some incense." ' (All these things, with the exception of the incense, had been mentioned in the letter that was about to be sent.)

So God, Who had guided the kings to go with gifts to honour His Son, also inspired this noble and holy lady to go with gifts to honour His best-beloved servant on the day of his death, which was rather the day of his true birth. Then Lady Jacoba prepared the food that the holy Father had wished to eat, but he could only take a little of it because he was steadily growing weaker and drawing nearer to death. She also had many candles made to burn before his most holy body after death, and from the cloth the friars made him the habit in which he was buried. But he told the friars to sew him in sack-cloth as a sign of holy Humility and of the Lady Poverty. And during the week in which Lady Jacoba arrived, our most holy Father passed away to the Lord.

PART XI

ON HIS LOVE FOR CREATURES, AND OF
CREATURES FOR HIM

113

*Firstly, on his especial love for hooded larks, because to him they were
an image of the good Religious.*

BEING completely absorbed in the love of God, blessed Francis
clearly perceived the goodness of God both within his own
soul, already endowed with perfect virtue, and in all created
things, so he therefore had an especial and profound love for
God's creatures, and especially for those which he thought of
as representing some truth about God or religion.

Above all birds he loved the little lark, known in the language
of the country as *lodola capellata* (the hooded lark). He used to
say of it, 'Sister lark has a hood like a Religious and is a humble
bird, for she walks contentedly along the road to find grain, and
even if she finds it among rubbish, she pecks it out and eats it.
As she flies she praises God very sweetly, like good Religious
who despise earthly things, whose *minds are set on the things of
heaven,* and whose constant purpose is to praise God. Her
plumage resembles the earth, and she sets an example to Religious not to wear fine and gaudy clothing, but cloth of a humble
price and colour, just as earth is inferior to the other elements.'

Because he saw these things in them, he always looked on
them with great pleasure, so it pleased God that these little birds
should give him a sign of affection at the hour of his death. For
late that Saturday evening, after Vespers on the night when he

passed away to the Lord, a great flight of larks assembled above the roof of the house where he lay. And they circled around it in the form of a wheel, singing sweetly as they flew and seeming to praise God.

114

How he wanted to persuade the Emperor to enact an especial law requiring everyone to provide generously for birds, cattle, asses, and the poor on Christmas Day.

WE who were with blessed Francis and write about these events testify that we have often heard him say, 'If I ever speak to the Emperor, I shall beg him for love of God and myself to enact an especial law, forbidding anyone to kill our sisters the larks or do them any harm. Similarly, all mayors of towns and lords of castles and villages should be obliged each year on the Nativity of our Lord to see that their people scatter wheat and other grain on the roads outside towns and villages, so that our sisters the larks and other birds may have food on such a solemn festival. And in reverence for the Son of God, Who with the most blessed Virgin Mary rested in a manger that night between an ox and an ass, anyone who owns an ox or an ass should be obliged to give them the choicest of fodder on Christmas Eve. And on Christmas Day the rich should give an abundance of good things to all the poor.'

For blessed Francis had a deeper veneration for the Nativity of our Lord than for other festivals, and he said, 'Since our Lord has been born for us, it is for us to accept salvation.' He wanted every Christian to rejoice in the Lord on that day, and for love of Him Who gave Himself for us, he wished everyone to provide generously not only for the poor, but for beasts and birds as well.

On the love and obedience of fire to blessed Francis when he was cauterized.

WHEN blessed Francis came to the hermitage of Fonte Colombo to undergo a cure for his eyes—which he did under obedience to the orders of the Lord Cardinal of Ostia and of Brother Elias the Minister General—the doctor came to visit him one day. When he had examined him, he told blessed Francis that he wished to make a cautery from the jaw up to the eyebrow of the weaker eye. But because Brother Elias had expressed a desire to be present when the doctor began the operation, blessed Francis did not wish the treatment to begin until Brother Elias's arrival. The Father was also much disturbed at being the object of so much attention, and wanted the Minister General to be responsible for giving instructions. But Elias had been delayed by much business, and when they had waited for him in vain, blessed Francis at length asked the doctor to proceed.

When the iron had been placed in the fire to make the cautery, blessed Francis was afraid that he might show weakness, and wishing to strengthen his resolution, spoke to the fire, saying, 'Brother Fire, so noble and useful among other creatures, be gentle to me in this hour, for I have always loved you and will always do so for love of Him Who created you. I pray our Creator, Who made us, to temper your heat so that I can bear it.' And as he ended this prayer, he blessed the fire with the sign of the cross. At this moment we who were with him were so overcome with pity and compassion for him that we all fled, and left him alone with the doctor. When the cautery was completed we came back, and he said, 'Faint-hearts! Men of little faith! Why did you run away? I assure you that I felt no pain or heat from the fire. Indeed, if this cautery does not satisfy the doctor, let him do it again.' The doctor was amazed at his words, and said, 'My brothers, I would be afraid to apply so drastic a cautery to the strongest man, let alone to one who is so frail and ill. But he did not flinch or betray the least sign of pain.' Although all the veins from the ear to the eyebrow had been seared, this operation did not benefit him, nor did a second, when another doctor pierced both his ears with a red-hot iron.

It is not surprising that fire and other creatures sometimes obeyed and revered him, for we who were with him often saw how much he loved them, and what pleasure he took in them. Indeed, his spirit was stirred by such love and compassion for them that he would not allow them to be treated without respect. He used to speak to them as though they were rational creatures with such inward and outward joy that at times he was rapt in ecstasy.

116

How he would not allow the fire that had burned his under-linen to be extinguished.

AMONG all lesser created things blessed Francis had an especial love for fire, because of its beauty and usefulness, and would not allow it to be denied its natural function. Once while he was sitting close to the fire, his linen underclothes caught fire near the knee without his notice; and although he felt the heat, he was unwilling to put out the flames. Seeing his clothes alight, his companion ran to put out the flame, but blessed Francis would not allow it, saying, 'Dearest brother, do not hurt Brother Fire!' So his companion ran to the friar who was Guardian and brought him to blessed Francis, and against his wishes the Guardian beat out the flames. But so dearly did he love fire that, however pressing the need, he would never put out a flame, whether a lamp or a candle. And he would not allow any friar to throw burning or smouldering wood from one place to another, as is often done; he wished them to lay it properly on the ground out of reverence for God Who created it.

How he would never again use a fleece because he had not allowed Brother Fire to burn it.

ONE day, while he was observing Lent on Mount La Verna, his companion laid a fire at dinner time in the cell where he used to eat. When the fire was alight he went to fetch blessed Francis from another cell where he was at prayer, and took a missal with him in order to read him the Gospel for the day; for whenever he had been unable to hear Mass, the Father always wished to hear the Gospel for the day read before his meal.

On returning to the cell where he had lit a fire to cook the meal, the friar found that the flames had already reached the roof and were burning it. He did his best to extinguish the flames, but could not do so single-handed, and blessed Francis was unwilling to help him. His only action was to pick up a fleece that he used as a covering at night, and go away with it into a wood. But when the other friars, who were living some distance away, saw his cell burning down, they ran at once and put out the fire. Some time later blessed Francis returned for a meal, and when he had eaten, he said to his companions, 'I shall not use this fleece over me again, for in my avarice I would not allow Brother Fire to consume it.'

On his especial love for water, rocks, wood, and flowers.

NEXT to fire he had an especial love for water, because it symbolizes holy penitence and tribulation, and at Baptism the soul is cleansed from its stains and receives its first purification. So whenever he washed his hands he chose a place where the water would not be trodden underfoot as it fell to the ground. For the same reason, whenever he had to walk over rocks, he trod reverently and fearfully, out of love for Christ Who is called *The Rock*: so whenever he recited the psalm *Thou wilt set me high up on a rock*, he used to say with great reverence and devotion, *Thou hast set me up at the foot of the rock*.

He told the friar who cut and chopped wood for the fire that he must never cut down the whole tree, but remove branches in such a way that part of the tree remained intact, out of love for Christ, Who willed to accomplish our salvation on the wood of the cross.

In the same way he told the friar who cared for the gardens not to cultivate all the ground for vegetables, but to set aside a plot to grow flowers to bloom in their season, out of love for Him Who is called *The Rose on the plain and the Lily on the mountain slopes*. Indeed, he told the brother-gardener that he should always make a pleasant flower-garden, and cultivate every variety of fragrant herb and flowering plant, so that all who saw the herbs and flowers would be moved to praise God. For every creature proclaims, 'God made me for your sake, O man.'

We who were with him have seen him take inward and outward delight in almost every creature, and when he handled or looked at them his spirit seemed to be in heaven rather than on earth. And not long before his death, in gratitude for the many consolations that he had received through creatures, he composed *The Praises of the Lord in His Creatures*, in order to stir the hearts of those who heard them to the praise of God, and to move men to praise the Lord Himself in His creatures.

119

How he praised the sun and fire above all other creatures.

ABOVE all creatures unendowed with reason he had a particular love for the sun and for fire. He used to say, 'At dawn, when the sun rises, all men should praise God, Who created him for our use, and through him gives light to our eyes by day. And at nightfall every man should praise God for Brother Fire, by whom He gives light to our eyes in the darkness. For we are all blind, and by these two brothers of ours God gives light to our eyes, so we should give special praise to our Creator for these and other creatures that serve us day by day.'

Blessed Francis himself always offered this praise until the day of his death, and even when his illness grew more serious he used to sing *The Praises of the Lord in His Creatures* which he had composed. Later he asked his companions to sing them, so that their occupation with the praises of God might make them forget the bitterness of his suffering and disease. And since in Holy Scripture the Lord Himself is called *The Sun of Justice*, and because blessed Francis thought the sun the loveliest of God's creatures and most worthy of comparison with Him, he gave its name to the *Praises of God in His Creatures* which he had written when the Lord had assured him of His Kingdom. And he called them *The Song of Brother Sun*.

120

The Praises that he composed when the Lord assured him of His kingdom.

Most High, Almighty, good Lord,
Thine be the praise, the glory, the honour,
And all blessing.

To Thee alone, Most High, are they due,
And no man is worthy
To speak Thy Name.

Praise to Thee, my Lord, for all Thy creatures,
Above all Brother Sun
Who brings us the day and lends us his light.

Lovely is he, radiant with great splendour,
And speaks to us of Thee,
O Most High.

Praise to Thee, my Lord, for Sister Moon and the stars
Which Thou hast set in the heavens,
Clear, precious, and fair.

Praise to Thee, my Lord, for Brother Wind,
For air and cloud, for calm and all weather,
By which Thou supportest life in all Thy creatures.

Praise to Thee, my Lord, for Sister Water,
Who is so useful and humble,
Precious and pure.

Praise to Thee, my Lord, for Brother Fire,
By whom Thou lightest the night;
He is lovely and pleasant, mighty and strong.

Praise to Thee, my Lord, for our sister Mother Earth
Who sustains and directs us,
And brings forth varied fruits, and coloured flowers, and plants.

Praise to Thee, my Lord, for those who pardon one another
For love of Thee, and endure
Sickness and tribulation.

Blessed are they who shall endure it in peace,
For they shall be crowned by Thee,
O Most High.

Praise to Thee, my Lord, for our Sister bodily Death
From whom no man living may escape:
Woe to those who die in mortal sin.

Blessed are they who are found in Thy most holy will,
For the second death cannot harm them.

Praise and bless my Lord,
Thank Him and serve Him
With great humility.

Part XII

ON HIS DEATH, AND THE JOY THAT HE SHOWED WHEN HE KNEW THAT DEATH WAS DRAWING NEAR

121

Firstly, how he answered Brother Elias when the latter reproved him for his obvious joy.

WHEN he was lying ill in the episcopal palace at Assisi, the hand of God appeared to press upon him more heavily than usual, and the people of Assisi feared that if he were to die during the night, the friars might take his holy body and carry it to some other place. So they arranged to post men on guard around the walls of the palace each night.

To comfort his soul and strengthen his resolution during the violent attacks of pain that constantly racked him, blessed Francis often asked his companions to sing him the *Praises of the Lord* during the day, and to do so during the night to edify and console those who were keeping watch outside the palace on his account.

Seeing that blessed Francis was comforted and rejoicing in the Lord in this way despite his great pain, Brother Elias said to him, 'Dearest Brother, the great joy shown by you and your companions gives me great comfort and edification. But the people of this city venerate you as a saint, and are well aware that you will soon die of your incurable disease; so when they hear the *Praises* sung day and night they are likely to say to themselves, "How can this man show so much joy when he is about to die? He ought to be preparing himself for death." '

Blessed Francis said to him, 'Do you remember the vision that you saw at Foligno, when you told me that it had been revealed to you that I had only two years to live? Before you had this vision, by the grace of God Who implants all good things in our hearts and inspires the words of the faithful, I often meditated upon my end both by day and by night. And after you had that vision, I was even more careful to give daily thought to my death.' Then he continued in great fervour of spirit, 'Brother, allow me in my infirmities to *rejoice in the Lord* and in His praises, for by the grace and assistance of the Holy Spirit I am so united and conjoined to my Lord that by His mercy I may rightly rejoice in Him, the Most High.'

122

How he persuaded a doctor to tell him how long he had to live.

AT that time a doctor from Arrezzo named John Buono, a close friend of blessed Francis, came to visit him in the bishop's palace, and blessed Francis asked him, 'Finiate, what do you think about this dropsical disease of mine?' (For he would never call him by his proper name (*Buono-Good*), because he never addressed anyone who was called Good by their name out of reverence for the Lord, Who said, *God is good, and He only.* For the same reason he would never call anyone Father or Master, or use these titles in a letter, out of reverence for our Lord, Who said, *Nor are you to call any man on earth your father. Nor are you to be called teachers.*)

The doctor said to him, 'Brother, God willing, all will be well with you.' Again blessed Francis said to him, 'Tell me the truth. What is your real opinion? Don't be afraid to tell me, for by God's grace I am not such a coward as to fear death. By the grace and help of the Holy Spirit I am so united to my Lord that I am equally content to die or to live.'

Then the doctor told him frankly, 'Father, according to our

medical knowledge your disease is incurable, and it is my belief that you will die either at the end of September or in early October.' Then blessed Francis, lying on his bed, most reverently and devoutly stretched out his hands to God, and with great joy of mind and body, said, 'Welcome, Sister Death.'

123

*How, as soon as he heard of his approaching death, he ordered the
Praises that he had written to be sung.*

AFTER this, one of the friars said to him, 'Father, your life and teaching have been, and remain, a light and mirror not only to your friars but to the whole Church, and your death will be the same. And although your passing will be an occasion of sorrow and grief to your brethren and many others, to you it will bring consolation and infinite joy. For you will pass from great toil to great repose, from many sorrows and temptations to eternal peace, from earthly poverty, which you have always loved and observed perfectly, to true and boundless riches, from death in this world to everlasting life in which you will see the Lord your God face to face, and gaze on Him Whom you have loved with such fervent love and desire in this life.' Then he said frankly, 'Father, you already know for certain that, unless the Lord sends you healing from heaven, your disease is incurable, and the doctors have said that you have only a short while to live. But I have spoken as I have to strengthen your spirit, so that you may continue to rejoice in the Lord both inwardly and outwardly. So the friars and others who visit you will always find you rejoicing in the Lord, and both to those who see it and others who hear of it after your passing not only your life and teaching but your death itself will be an everlasting memorial.'

Although blessed Francis was in greater pain from his diseases than usual, when he heard that Sister Death was fast approaching, he was filled with fresh joy, and praised the Lord in great fervour

151

of spirit, saying, 'If it be my Lord's pleasure that I should die soon, call me Brother Angelo and Brother Leo, and let them sing to me of Sister Death.' And when these two friars, filled with sorrow and grief, had come to him, they sang with many tears the *Song of Brother Sun* and the other creatures which the Saint had written. And before the last verse of the Song, he added these lines on Sister Death:

> Praised be Thou, my Lord, for Sister Bodily Death
> From whom no man living may escape.
>
> Woe to those who die in mortal sin,
> And blessed are those who are found in Thy most holy will,
> For the second death can do them no ill.

124

How he blessed the city of Assisi while he was being carried to die at S. Mary's.

THE most holy Father had now been informed by the Holy Spirit as well as by the doctors that his death was near. Hitherto he had been lodged in the bishop's palace, but when he felt himself growing steadily worse and his bodily powers failing, he asked to be carried on a litter to S. Mary of the Porziuncula, so that his bodily life should draw to its close in the place where his spiritual life and light had come into being.

When the brethren who were carrying him arrived at the hospice standing by the road half-way between Assisi and S. Mary's, he asked the bearers to set the litter on the ground. And although his long-standing and severe disease of the eyes had almost deprived him of sight, he had the litter turned to face the city of Assisi. Raising himself a little, he blessed the city, saying, 'Lord, it is said that in former days this city was the haunt of wicked men. But now it is clear that of Thine infinite mercy and in Thine own time Thou hast been pleased to shower especial and abundant favours upon it. Of Thy goodness alone Thou hast chosen it for Thyself, that it may become the home and dwelling of those who know Thee in truth and glorify Thy holy Name, and spread abroad the fragrance of a good report, of holy life, of true doctrine, and of evangelical perfection to all Christian people. I therefore beseech Thee, O Lord Jesus Christ, Father of mercies, that Thou wilt not remember our ingratitude, but ever be mindful of Thine abundant compassion which Thou hast showed towards it, that it may ever be the home and dwelling-place of those who know Thee in truth and glorify Thy blessed and most glorious Name for ever and ever. Amen.'

When he had ended his prayer, he was carried on to S. Mary's. There, on October the third, 1226, in the fortieth year of his life and after twenty years of perfect penitence, he departed to the Lord Jesus Christ, Whom he had loved with all his heart, with all his mind, with all his soul, and all his strength, with the most ardent desire and with utter devotion, following Him perfectly, hastening swiftly in His footsteps, and at last coming in the greatest glory to Him Who lives and reigns with the Father and the Holy Spirit for ever and ever. *Amen.*

Here ends the Mirror of Perfection,
which tells of the state of the Friar Minor,
and in which the perfection of his vocation and profession
may be seen accurately reflected.

All praise and glory to God the Father, and to the Son, and to the Holy Spirit.
ALLELUIA! ALLELUIA! ALLELUIA!
Honour and exaltation to His most blessed servant Francis.
ALLELUIA!
Amen.

THE WRITINGS OF S. FRANCIS

THE PRAYERS AND PRAISES
OF SAINT FRANCIS

I

A PARAPHRASE OF THE LORD'S PRAYER

This lovely prayer is found in all manuscripts, and is undoubtedly from the hand of the Saint. It is referred to in chapter 82 of the Mirror of Perfection, *where any friar guilty of idle talk is required to recite this Our Father and the Praises as penance. Saint Francis ordered them to be said at all the day and night Hours, and before the Office of the Blessed Virgin Mary.*

OUR FATHER,
most holy,
Creator,
Redeemer,
Saviour,
Comforter,

WHO ART IN HEAVEN,
in the Angels and Saints
enlightening them to knowledge of Thee,
for Thou, Lord, art Light;
inflaming them to love of Thee,
for Thou, Lord, art Love;
dwelling in them, and filling them with blessing,
for Thou, Lord, art the highest good,
the eternal good,
from Whom all good proceeds,
without Whom nothing is good.

157

HALLOWED BE THY NAME,
may it be glorified in us
by knowledge of Thee,
that we may perceive
the wideness of Thy blessings,
the extent of Thy promises,
the height of Thy majesty,
the depth of Thy judgements.

THY KINGDOM COME,
that Thou mayest reign in us
by Thy grace,
and bring us to Thy kingdom,
where the vision of Thee is revealed,
and Thy love made perfect,
that we may enter Thy blessed presence,
and enjoy Thee for ever.

THY WILL BE DONE IN EARTH
AS IT IS DONE IN HEAVEN,
that we may love Thee with all our heart,
ever thinking of Thee,
and desiring Thee with all our soul
and with all our mind;
directing all our intentions to Thee,
and seeking Thine honour in all things;
with all our strength
devoting every power and faculty
of mind and body to the service of Thy love,
and to no other end.

May we also love our neighbours as ourselves,
drawing them to love of Thee
with all our power;

S. CLARE'S GARDEN AT SAN DAMIANO

Where S. Francis first sang the Canticle of the Sun

delighting in the good of others
as in our own,
sharing in their troubles,
and giving no offence to any.

GIVE US THIS DAY OUR DAILY BREAD,
which is Thy beloved Son
Jesus Christ our Lord,
in the remembrance, understanding, and reverence
of the love that He bore us,
and for the things that He said, did, and endured
for our sakes.

AND FORGIVE US OUR TRESPASSES
through Thine Infinite mercy,
and by virtue of the Passion
of Thy beloved Son our Lord
Jesus Christ,
and through the merits and prayers
of the most blessed Virgin Mary
and of all Thine elect.

AS WE FORGIVE THEM THAT TRESPASS AGAINST US,
and since we do not forgive fully
do Thou, Lord, enable us to forgive fully
so that we may truly love our enemies
for Thy sake,
and pray them devoutly to Thee,
not returning evil for evil,
but seeking to serve all men in Thee.

AND LEAD US NOT INTO TEMPTATION,
hidden or open,
sudden or persistent,

F

BUT DELIVER US FROM EVIL,
past,
present,
and to come.
AMEN.

II

THE PRAISES OF THE TRINITY

HOLY, Holy, Holy, Lord God Almighty,
Who is and Who was and Who is to come.
Let us praise and exalt Him above all for ever.
Worthy art Thou, O Lord our God, to receive praise, glory,
honour and blessing.
Let us praise and exalt Him above all for ever.
Worthy is the Lamb that was slain to receive power and divinity,
wisdom and strength, honour, glory, and blessing.

Let us praise and exalt Him above all for ever.
Let us bless the Father, the Son, and the Holy Spirit,
Let us praise and exalt Him above all for ever.
All ye works of the Lord, bless ye the Lord.
Let us praise and exalt Him above all for ever.
Praise God, all ye His servants, and ye that fear Him, both small
and great.
Let us praise and exalt Him above all for ever.
Let heaven and earth praise His glory.
And every creature that is in heaven, and on earth, and under
the earth.
Let us praise and exalt Him above all for ever.
Glory be to the Father, and to the Son, and to the Holy Spirit,
As it was in the beginning, is now, and ever shall be,
world without end.
Amen.

160

ALMIGHTY, most holy, most high and supreme God, highest good, all good, wholly good, Who alone art good; We offer Thee all praise, all glory, all thanks, all honour, all blessing, and will ever ascribe all good to Thee. Amen.

III

THE SONG OF BROTHER SUN AND OF ALL CREATURES

Blind, weak, and in great pain, Saint Francis passed seven weeks in the summer of 1225 at San Damiano, where Saint Clare had lovingly prepared for him a little hut of rush matting in the garden, in the hope that rest and quiet would assist his recovery. Despite great suffering he never lost his serenity and joy, and receiving one night an assurance of future blessedness, he composed this canticle of praise in his native Italian, and taught the brethren to sing it to the people when they preached. Not long afterwards the Bishop and Mayor of Assisi had a serious dispute, and the Saint composed the stanza 'Praise to Thee, my Lord, for those who pardon one another,' and sent some friars to sing it before them to effect a reconciliation. Two years later, at the approach of death, he called on Brother Leo and Brother Angelo to sing the Canticle to him, and added the stanza, 'Praised be my Lord for our Sister Death.'

It should perhaps be mentioned that the Italian per *can mean both* for *and* by, *which makes it uncertain whether Francis is praising God* for *His creatures, or asking that God may be praised* by *His creatures, as in the* Benedicite. *The general sense, especially those of the last stanzas, seems to favour the first meaning.*

Most High, Almighty, good Lord,
Thine be the praise, the glory, the honour,
And all blessing.

161

To Thee alone, Most High, are they due,
And no man is worthy
To speak Thy Name.

Praise to Thee, my Lord, for all Thy creatures,
Above all Brother Sun
Who brings us the day and lends us his light.

Lovely is he, radiant with great splendour,
And speaks to us of Thee,
O Most High.

Praise to Thee, my Lord, for Sister Moon and the stars
Which Thou hast set in the heavens,
Clear, precious, and fair.

Praise to Thee, my Lord, for Brother Wind,
For air and cloud, for calm and all weather,
By which Thou supportest life in all Thy creatures.

Praise to Thee, my Lord, for Sister Water,
Who is so useful and humble,
Precious and pure.

Praise to Thee, my Lord, for Brother Fire,
By whom Thou lightest the night;
He is lovely and pleasant, mighty and strong.

Praise to Thee, my Lord, for our sister Mother Earth
Who sustains and directs us,
And brings forth varied fruits, and coloured flowers, and plants.

Praise to Thee, my Lord, for those who pardon one another
For love of Thee, and endure
Sickness and tribulation.

Blessed are they who shall endure it in peace,
For they shall be crowned by Thee,
O Most High.

Praise to Thee, my Lord, for our Sister bodily Death
From whom no man living may escape:
Woe to those who die in mortal sin.

Blessed are they who are found in Thy most holy will,
For the second death cannot harm them.

Praise and bless my Lord,
Thank Him and serve Him
With great humility.

IV

SAINT FRANCIS'S BLESSING OF BROTHER LEO

*Both Saint Bonaventura and Thomas of Celano tell us that shortly
after the holy Father had received the imprint of the sacred Stigmata
he called on Brother Leo to bring him a pen and parchment, so that he
could write down some praises of God. As he was writing it seems
to have entered his understanding heart that there was nothing in the
world that Leo wanted more dearly than some sacred words written in
his master's hand. So having written the Praises, Francis added a
blessing for Brother Leo in the words of Holy Scripture, saying,
'Take this parchment and keep it carefully to the day of your death.
It will immediately put every temptation to flight.'*

THE Lord bless you and keep you.
May He show you His face and be merciful to you.
May He turn His countenance to you, and give you peace.
The Lord bless you, ✠ Brother Leo.

The original, worn and creased by its years in the breast of Brother Leo's robe, is reverently preserved at Assisi. In the margin Leo has written, 'Two years before his death, Saint Francis fasted on Mount La Verna in honour of the blessed Virgin Mary, Mother of the Lord, and of S. Michael the Archangel, which fast lasted from the feast of the Assumption until the feast of S. Michael in September. And the hand of the Lord rested upon him. And after the vision and the words of the seraph, and the imprinting of the wounds of Christ on his body, he wrote these praises on the other side of the parchment, and with his own hand gave thanks to God for the favour conferred on him.' A little way below is added, 'Blessed Francis wrote this blessing with his own hand for me, Brother Leo.'

THOU alone art holy, Lord God, Who doest wondrous things.
Thou art strong. Thou art great. Thou art the Most High.
Thou art the Almighty King, the Holy Father, King of heaven and earth.
Thou art Trinity and Unity, O Lord God, All Goodness.
Thou art Good, All Good, the Supreme Good,
Lord God, living and true.
Thou art Charity and Love. Thou art Wisdom.
Thou art Humility. Thou art Patience.
Thou art Serenity. Thou art Peace.
Thou art Joy and Gladness. Thou art Justice and Temperance.
Thou art our Wealth, our Treasure, and our Satisfaction.
Thou art Beauty. Thou art Clemency.
Thou art our Protector. Thou art our Guardian and Defender.
Thou art Strength. Thou art Refreshment.
Thou art our Hope. Thou art our Trust.
Thou art our Delight. Thou art Eternal Life,
Great and wondrous Lord,
Almighty God,
Merciful Saviour.

V

THE PRAISES OF THE BLESSED VIRGIN MARY

This is described in some manuscripts as a 'Praise of the virtues with which the Blessed Virgin was adorned, and which should adorn a holy soul.'

HAIL, holy Lady, most holy Queen, Mary Mother of God, who remainest ever-Virgin, chosen by the most holy Father in heaven, Who with the most holy and beloved Son and the Holy Spirit hallowed thee, in whom abode and still abides the fullness of grace and every blessing.

Hail, His Palace. Hail, His Dwelling. Hail, His Home. Hail, His Robe. Hail, His Handmaid. Hail, His Mother. And hail, all ye holy virtues which by the grace and illumination of the Holy Spirit are poured into the hearts of the faithful, so that you may transform them from unbelief to faith in God.

VI

IN PRAISE OF THE VIRTUES

WHICH ADORNED THE HOLY VIRGIN, AND WHICH SHOULD ADORN A HOLY SOUL

This is probably the praise of the virtues mentioned by Thomas of Celano in his second Life (Chap. 189).

HAIL, Queen Wisdom,
The Lord keep thee and thy holy sister, pure Simplicity.
Hail, Lady holy Poverty,
The Lord keep thee and thy holy sister Humility.
Hail, Lady holy Charity,
The Lord keep thee and thy holy sister Obedience.

Hail, all ye most holy Virtues,
May the Lord keep you,
For it is from Him alone that you derive.

No one in all the world may possess a single one of you unless he first dies to self. He who possesses one and does not offend against the others possesses all. But he who offends against one possesses none and offends against all.

Each of the Virtues overcomes vices and sins. Holy Wisdom overcomes Satan and all his malice. Pure and holy Simplicity overcomes all the wisdom of this world and all carnal wisdom. Holy Poverty overcomes all the greed, avarice, and desires of this world. Holy Humility overcomes pride, together with all who love this world, and all the things of this world. Holy Charity overcomes all the temptations of the devil and the flesh, and all the fears of the flesh. Holy Obedience overcomes all carnal desires, and keeps the body under discipline, ready to obey its brother the spirit; it renders a man submissive to all things in this world, not only to men but even to wild beasts, so that they may do their will with him in whatsoever way God may permit.

VII

TWO PRAYERS

Of the prayer 'Absorbeat, quaeso, Domine . . .' Luke Wadding in his 'Annales Minorum' (pub. between 1625–1654) says, 'That Francis is the author of this prayer is attested by Saint Bernadine in his Sermon LX, and by Ubertino (Ubertino da Casale, d. 1338) in his "Arbor Vitae Crucifixae."'

O LORD Jesus Christ, I pray Thee that the fiery and honey-sweet power of Thy love may detach my soul from everything under heaven, so that I may die for love of Thy love, Who out of love for Thy people didst die on the tree of the Cross.

This prayer concludes the Saint's 'Letter to the Chapter General and all the friars,' and crystallizes his desire that the Order remain loyal to its original spirit and purpose.

ALMIGHTY, eternal, just, and merciful God, grant us wretched sinners for Thy sake to do what we know to be Thy will, and always to will whatsoever pleases Thee; so that, inwardly cleansed and enlightened, and warmed by the fire of the Holy Spirit, we may be enabled to follow in the footsteps of Thy Son, our Lord Jesus Christ, and by grace alone come to Thee, O Most High, Who in perfect Trinity and undivided Unity livest and reignest in glory, God Almighty, for ever and ever.

VIII

AN ANTIPHON OF THE BLESSED VIRGIN

HOLY Virgin Mary, there is none like thee among women born into this world, daughter and handmaid of the most high King, the heavenly Father, Mother of our most holy Lord Jesus Christ, Spouse of the Holy Spirit. Pray for us, with Saint Michael the Archangel, all the powers of heaven, and all the Saints to thy beloved and most holy Son, our Lord and Master.

(From the Office of the Passion.)

THE COUNSELS OF THE HOLY FATHER
SAINT FRANCIS

The Counsels of Saint Francis are accepted as authentic by all authorities, but we have no means of knowing when they were written, or the exact circumstances that called for them. It has been suggested that they are pronouncements made by the Saint at various Pentecost Chapters and recorded at the time. But whatever their original background may have been, they faithfully reflect the spirit and outlook of Saint Francis.

1

On the Body of Christ.

Our Lord Jesus Christ said to His disciples, *I am the Way; I am Truth and Life; nobody can come to the Father except through Me. If you had learned to recognize Me, you would have learned to recognize My Father too. From now onwards you are to recognize Him; you have seen Him. Philip said to Him, Lord, let us see the Father; that is all we ask. Jesus said to him, What, Philip, here am I, Who have been all this while in your company; hast thou not learned to recognize Me yet? Whoever has seen Me, has seen the Father.*

The Father *dwells in unapproachable light,* and *God is a spirit,* and *no man has ever seen God.* Because God is a spirit, He cannot be seen except in the spirit; for only *the spirit gives life; the flesh is of no avail.* Nor is the Son, Who is equal to the Father, seen by any but the Father and the Holy Spirit. Therefore, all who have seen the Lord Jesus Christ in His Humanity without seeing or believing in His spirit and divinity, and without believing that He is the Son of God, are condemned. In the same way, those who see the Sacrament of Christ's Body, which is hallowed by the words of our Lord at the altar in the hands of His priest under the forms of bread and wine, and who do not recognize His spirit and divinity, believing It to be truly the most holy Body and Blood of our Lord Jesus Christ, are condemned out of the mouth of Almighty God Himself, Who testifies: *This is My Body and Blood of the New Testament;* and *Whoso eateth My Flesh and drinketh My Blood hath eternal life.*

So he who has the spirit of God, which dwells in those who have faith in Him, is he who rightly receives the most holy Body and Blood of the Lord. All others, who possess nothing of this spirit and yet presume to receive the Sacrament, *eat and drink damnation to themselves.* Therefore we read: *Sons of men, will your hearts always be hardened?* Why do you not acknowledge the truth, and believe in the Son of God? See how He humbles Himself daily, for just as He descended from His royal throne into the Virgin's womb, so does He come to us day by day in humble form. Daily He descends from the bosom of the Father to the altar in the hands of the priest. And as He once appeared to the holy Apostles in true flesh, so does He reveal Himself to us in the hallowed bread. And as they gazed on Him with their bodily eyes and saw only His human nature, although when they contemplated Him with the eyes of the spirit they knew Him to be God, so we, as we look on the bread and wine with our bodily eyes, firmly believe and know that here are His most holy Body and Blood, living and true. This is the way in which the Lord is always present with His faithful ones, as He Himself promises: *I am with you all through the days that are coming, until the consummation of the world.*

2

On the evil of self-will.

THE Lord said to Adam: *Thou mayest eat thy fill of all the trees in the garden except the tree which brings knowledge of good and evil;*

if ever thou eatest of this, thy doom is death. So Adam was permitted to eat of every tree in the garden, and so long as he did not disobey, he did not sin. For a man eats of the tree of the knowledge of good when he directs his will to his own ends, and boasts about the good that God works through him. By this means, through the instigation of the devil and his own disobedience to the command of God, the good fruit is transformed into the fruit of the knowledge of evil, and for this he has to suffer the penalty.

3

On perfect and imperfect obedience.

Our Lord says in the Gospel: *None of you can be My disciple if he does not take leave of that he possesses,* and, *The man who tries to save his life shall lose it.* The man who renounces all his possessions and loses himself body and soul is the man who surrenders himself to obedience in the hands of his superior. Therefore, provided that it is good and is not contrary to the will of his superior, all that he does or says is true obedience. And if, while thus under obedience, he should see things that seem better and more profitable to his soul than those commanded by his superior, let him surrender his will to God in sacrifice and take care to carry out the orders of his superior. For this is true and loving obedience, acceptable to God and one's neighbour.

Should a superior give an order which is against the conscience of a subject, he is not obliged to obey, but he may not leave him; and if his refusal brings persecution on him, he must love his persecutors all the more for God's sake. For one who would suffer persecution rather than separate himself from his brethren is living in true and perfect obedience, because he is *laying down his life for his friends.* But there are many Religious who, claiming to see a better course of action than that ordered by their superiors, *look back* and *return to the vomit* of their own self-will. Such

170

men are guilty of manslaughter, because their evil example causes the loss of many souls.

4

That no man may take upon himself the office of superior.

I have not come to have service done Me, but to serve others, says the Lord. Those who are appointed to rule over others may not boast of their position any more than if they were to be assigned to the duty of washing their brethren's feet. And if they are more disturbed about the possibility of losing their position than they would be about losing the duty of foot-washing, they will expose their souls to great danger.

5

That no man may boast save in the Cross of our Lord.

CONSIDER, O man, to what sublime a dignity the Lord has raised you, for He has created and formed you in the image of His beloved Son in your bodily nature, and in the likeness of Him in the spirit. All creatures under heaven serve, acknowledge, and obey their Creator better than you. Even the devils did not crucify Him, but you yourself have crucified Him and still do so by your delight in wickedness and sin. So what have you got to boast about? Were you so wise and clever that you possessed all knowledge, understood all languages, and pierced the mysteries of the heavens by your cunning, you could not boast about these things, for a single devil knows more about heaven and earth than all men put together, although there have been some men to whom God granted a special knowledge of sublime wisdom. And if you were the most handsome and wealthy of men, or if you could work wonders, or cast out devils, none of these things would avail you; you cannot claim credit for them or boast about them. But we may *boast of our humiliations*, and delight to bear the Cross of our Lord Jesus Christ day by day.

6

On the following of Christ.

MY brothers, let us think of the Good Shepherd, Who endured the Passion and Cross in order to save His sheep. Our Lord's sheep have followed Him in trouble, persecution and disgrace, in hunger and thirst, in temptation and other hardships, and by so doing have received from their Lord everlasting life. It therefore brings great disgrace on us servants of God that the Saints have done great things while we hope to win honour and fame merely by talking and preaching about them.

7

That knowledge should be followed by holy deeds.

THE Apostle Paul says, *The written law inflicts death, whereas the spiritual law brings life.* Those killed by the letter are those who only want to know the words of Christ in order to appear wiser and more learned than others, and to amass a great fortune to bestow on their families and friends. Even Religious are killed by the letter if they are not prepared to follow the spirit of the word of God, but are content merely to know it and explain it to others. But those who receive life from the spirit of the word of God are those who do not take every word that they study in its literal sense, but by their own word and example ascribe it to God most High, the Source of all good.

8

On avoiding the sin of envy.

THE Apostle Paul says, *No one can say 'Jesus is Lord' except through the Holy Spirit*, and, *An innocent man is nowhere to be found.* So whoever envies his brother because of the good that the Lord says or does through him is near to committing the sin of blasphemy, for his envy is against God most High Himself, Who is the Source and Author of all good.

9

On love.

OUR Lord says in the Gospel, *Love your enemies.* One who truly loves his enemy does not bear malice for any injury that he has received from him. Because he loves God he grieves for the sin on the other's soul, and shows his love by his actions.

10

On bodily mortification.

THERE are many people who always blame an enemy or a neighbour whenever they themselves do wrong or suffer some hurt. This is not just, for everyone has his enemy in his own power, that is, his own body, by which he sins. Blessed is the servant who keeps such an enemy constantly under his control, and wisely guards himself against him. For so long as he does this, no other enemy, visible or invisible, can harm him.

11

How no one is corrupted by another's evil.

NOTHING should be more displeasing to a servant of God than sin. If another person sins in some way, and the servant of God is distressed and angry about it, except through charity, he is *storing up retribution* for himself. But the servant of God who is not angry or distressed by anything whatsoever is living rightly

173

and without sin. And blessed is the man who retains nothing for himself, but *gives back to Caesar what is Caesar's, and to God what is God's.*

12

On recognizing the spirit of God.

A SERVANT of God may recognize whether he has the spirit of God in this way: if, when God performs any good through him his natural feelings are not puffed up—for the flesh is always the enemy of all good—and if he always remembers his own unworthiness, and regards himself as the least of all men.

13

On patience.

A SERVANT of God cannot know the extent of his patience and humility so long as all goes well with him. But when a time comes that those who should treat him well do the opposite, then he shows the true extent of his patience and humility, and no more.

14

On poverty of spirit.

Blessed are the poor in spirit; the kingdom of heaven is theirs. There are many who are regular in saying their prayers and Offices, and who discipline their bodies by fasts and austerities. But if a single word is uttered that offends them, or if they are deprived of anything, they are immediately provoked and offended. People of this sort are not *poor in spirit,* for one who is truly poor in spirit despises himself and shows charity towards those who *strike him in the face.*

15

On those who love peace.

Blessed are the peacemakers; they shall be counted the children of God.
True lovers of peace are those who, in all their sufferings upon
earth, remain at peace in mind and body for the love of Jesus
Christ.

16

On pureness of heart.

Blessed are the clean in heart; they shall see God. The clean in heart
are those who despise earthly things and aspire to heavenly. They
never cease to adore and see the Lord God, the living and the
true, with a clean heart and soul.

17

On the humble servant of God.

BLESSED is the servant who does not take greater pleasure in the
good which God says or does through him than that which He
does through others. When anyone wants to receive more
from his neighbour than he himself is prepared to give to the
Lord his God, he is guilty of sin.

18

On compassion towards our neighbour.

BLESSED is the man who helps his neighbour in trouble, just as
he would wish to be helped in like circumstances.

19

On the blessed and the unworthy servant.

BLESSED is the servant who regards all that he has as belonging to God; for whosoever retains anything for his own use *hides his Master's money;* and *will lose even what he thinks his own.*

20

On the good and humble Religious.

BLESSED is the servant who does not esteem himself as better when he is praised and promoted by men than when they look on him as vile, stupid, and contemptible; for whatever a man is in the sight of God, that he is, and no more. Woe to the Religious who is raised to high office by his fellows, but refuses to relinquish it. And blessed is the servant who is promoted by no desire of his own, and always desires to remain at the feet of others.

21

On the blessed and the foolish Religious.

BLESSED is the Religious whose sole joy and delight is in the most holy words and works of God, and thus leads men to the love of God with joy and gladness. And woe to the Religious who loves idle and foolish chatter, and thus leads men to laughter.

22

On the foolish and talkative Religious

BLESSED is the servant who does not speak in the hope of gain, does not discuss all his affairs, and is not eager to talk, but wisely weighs his words and replies. Woe to the Religious who does not hide the favours that God has shown him within his heart, and who does not show proof of them in his behaviour, but wants to tell everyone about them in hope of some gain. In so doing he has *already had his reward*, and those who listen to him reap little benefit.

23

On true discipline.

BLESSED is the servant who accepts instruction, accusation, and reproof from another as patiently as he would from himself. Blessed is the servant who accepts rebuke with courtesy, obeys respectfully, confesses humbly, and makes amends gladly. Blessed is the servant who is not in a hurry to excuse himself, but humbly accepts shame and reproach for a fault even when he is not to blame.

24

On true humility.

BLESSED is the man who is as humble among his subjects as among his superiors. Blessed is the servant who is always amenable to the rod of correction. The *faithful and wise servant* is one who does immediate penance for his misdeeds, both inwardly by contrition and outwardly by confession and active reparation.

25

On true love.

BLESSED is the man who loves his brother as much when he is ill and unable to help him as when he is well and able to do so.

177

Blessed is the man who loves and respects his brother when he is absent as when he is present, and never says anything behind his back that he could not in charity say to his face.

26

How servants of God should respect the clergy.

Blessed is the servant who is loyal to the clergy who live good lives and observe the laws of the holy Roman Church. And woe to those who despise them, for even when clergy are sinners, no man should judge them, since God reserves their judgement to Himself. For since their office is concerned with the most holy Body and Blood of our Lord Jesus Christ, which they receive and they alone may administer to others, it is higher than all others, so that any offence against them is more serious than those committed against other men in this world.

27

On the virtues which banish vices.

Where there is charity and wisdom, there is neither fear nor ignorance.
Where there is patience and humility, there is neither anger nor vexation.
Where there is poverty with joy, there is neither greed nor avarice.
Where there is peace and meditation, there is neither anxiety nor doubt.
Where the fear of the Lord stands guard, there the enemy finds no entry.
Where there is mercy and moderation, there is neither indulgence nor harshness.

28

On concealing God's favours, lest they be lost.

BLESSED is the servant who *lays up* the favours that God has shown him as *treasure in heaven*, and has no wish to disclose them to others in the hope of some advantage; for the Most High will reveal His workings to whomsoever He pleases. Blessed is the servant who keeps the secrets of the Lord locked away in his heart.

THE LETTERS

A LETTER ADDRESSED TO ALL THE FAITHFUL

*As its contents indicate, this letter was written during the Saint's
latter years, when, much to his grief, his weakness made it impossible
for him to travel the roads as an evangelist. This long letter was
clearly intended to be circulated among the friars and read by them
to their listeners as a personal Encyclical. It deals with reverence for
the Sacrament of the Altar, confession, self-discipline, and many other
practical matters.*

*TO all Christians, Religious, clergy and layfolk, men and women, to
all people throughout the world. Brother Francis, their servant and
subject, presents his services and respects, and wishes them the true
peace from heaven and sincere charity in our Lord.*

BEING the servant of all, it is my duty to serve everyone, and to
proclaim the gracious words of my Lord. So, knowing that my
bodily disease and weakness prevents my visiting you all in
person, I have decided to use this letter as my messenger in order
to bring to your minds the teachings of our Lord Jesus Christ,
the Word of the Father, and the words of the Spirit, which are
spirit and life.

God most high announced from heaven the coming of this
noble, holy, and glorious Word of the Father through His holy
Archangel to the holy and glorious Virgin Mary, in whose
womb He received the true flesh of our human nature and its
frailty. He Who was *so rich* willed to choose poverty with His
most blessed Mother. On the eve of His Passion He celebrated

the Passover with His disciples, and *taking bread, He gave thanks, and blessed and broke it, saying, 'Take, eat; this is My Body.'* And *taking the cup, He said, 'This is My Blood of the New Testament, which is to be shed for you and for many to the remission of sins.'* Then He prayed His Father, saying, *'Father, if it is possible let this chalice pass Me by.'* And *His sweat fell to the ground like thick drops of blood.* But He resigned His own will to the will of the Father, saying, *'Father, Thy will be done; not as I will, but as Thou wilt.'* It was the will of the Father that His blessed and glorious Son, Whom He gave to be born for us, should offer Himself through His own Blood as a Sacrifice and Victim upon the altar of the Cross. He was not to offer this Sacrifice for Himself, *by Whom all things came into being,* but for our sins, *leaving us His own example, that we should follow in His footsteps.* It is His will that we should be saved through Him, and that we should receive Him with a pure heart and chaste body. But few have any desire to receive Him and be saved through Him, although *His yoke is easy and His burden is light.*

(THE JOY OF SERVING GOD)

Those who have no desire to *taste and prove how gracious the Lord is,* who *prefer darkness to light,* and refuse to obey the commandments of God, are accursed. It is of such that the prophet says, *Thy curse lies on all who swerve from Thy covenant.* But how happy and blessed are those who love the Lord and do His will, as our Lord Himself says in the Gospel, *Thou shalt love the Lord thy God with thy whole soul, and thy neighbour as thyself.* Let us therefore love God and worship Him with a pure heart and a pure mind, for this is what He seeks above all else, saying, *true worshippers shall worship the Father in spirit and in truth.* For all who worship Him must worship Him in spirit and in truth. Let us offer Him our praises and prayers day and night, saying, *Our Father, Who art in heaven,* for we *ought to pray continually and never be discouraged.*

We must confess all our sins to a priest, and receive from him the Body and Blood of our Lord Jesus Christ. One who does not eat His Flesh and drink His Blood cannot enter *the kingdom of God*. But let a man eat and drink worthily, for if *he who eats and drinks unworthily* he *is eating and drinking damnation to himself, not recognizing the Lord's Body*; in other words, he makes no distinction between this and other food. Furthermore, we have to *yield the acceptable fruit of repentance*. And let us *love our neighbours as ourselves*; and if anyone is unwilling or unable to do this, let him at least refrain from doing them ill, but try to do them good.

(THE RIGHT USE OF AUTHORITY)

Those who have been given authority over others must exercise it with mercy, as they themselves hope for mercy from God. And let the man who shows no mercy be judged without mercy. We must be charitable, humble, and generous, for these things purify the soul from the stains of sin. For men leave behind all their possessions in this world, but they take with them the merits of their charity and almsgiving; for these the Lord will reward them generously.

(ON FASTING AND SPIRITUAL EXERCISES)

It is our duty to fast, to shun vices and sins, and to avoid over-indulgence in food and drink. We must also be loyal Catholics. We should pay frequent visits to churches, and respect the clergy—not so much for themselves, if they are sinners—but for their office and ministry of the most holy Body and Blood of our Lord Jesus Christ, which they plead in sacrifice upon the altar, and daily receive and administer to others. Let us all be clear in our minds that no one can be saved except through the Blood of our Lord Jesus Christ, and by His holy words (of consecration) which the priests alone may utter, for they alone may administer the Sacrament to others. Religious, who have renounced the world, are under a special obligation to do more and greater things for God, *and not to forget the other duties.*

(SELF–DISCIPLINE AND LOVE OF ENEMIES)

We must despise the body with its vices and sins, for our Lord says in the Gospel that *all vices and sins proceed from the heart*; and that we must *love our enemies, and do good to those who hate us.* We must obey the commands and teachings of our Lord Jesus Christ, and practice self-denial, subduing our bodies to accept the yoke of service and of holy obedience, as each of us has vowed to our Lord.

(THE SUPERIOR TO BE SERVANT OF ALL)

No one is obliged to obey an order which involves him in sin or wrong-doing. Let any man who is given authority and set over others regard himself as the least, and be the servant of all his brethren. He must show each of them the same kindness that he would wish to receive from them were he in their place. He must not lose his temper with an offending brother, but warn and encourage him kindly, with all patience and humility.

(AGAINST WORLDLY WISDOM)

We are not to be wise by the standards of this world, but simple, humble, and pure. We have to hold our bodies in contempt and subjection, for it is our own fault that we are all wretched and corrupted, *vile worms* as the Lord says through the prophet; *I am a poor worm and have no manhood left; I am a by-word to all, the laughing-stock of the rabble.* We should never want to dominate other people; rather should we be servants, *subject to every human authority for love of the Lord.* May the Spirit of the Lord rest upon all who do these things and persevere in them to the end. May He make His dwelling in them, so that they become *true sons of their Father in heaven*, Whose will they serve. They are spouses, brothers, and mothers of our Lord Jesus Christ. We are spouses of Christ when our soul is filled with faith and united to Jesus Christ by the Holy Spirit. We are His brothers when we *do the will of His Father, Who is in heaven*. We are His mothers when we conceive Him in our heart and body by pure love and a clean conscience, and when we bring Him forth by our holy actions, which are to give light and example to others.

(THE DIGNITY OF THE CHRISTIAN)

O how glorious, holy, and splendid a Father we have in heaven! O how sacred, wonderful, and lovable a Spouse we have in heaven! O how holy, beloved, kindly and humble, peaceable, sweet, loving, and supremely desirable a Brother we have in heaven! For He has *laid down His life for His sheep*, and has prayed the Father for us, saying, *Holy Father, keep them true to Thy Name, Thy gift to Me. Father, they belong to Thee; as all I have is Thine, and all Thou hast is Mine; and Thou gavest them to Me. I have given them Thy message. Now they have learned to recognize all the gifts Thou gavest Me as coming from Thee, and recognize it for truth that I came from Thee. It is for these I pray; I am not praying for the world; bless them and keep them holy. And I dedicate Myself for their sakes, that they too may be dedicated, and may be one as We are One. This, Father, is My desire that all those whom Thou hast entrusted to Me may be with Me where I am, so as to see My glory in Thy kingdom.*

(THE PRAISE OF GOD)

And because He has suffered so much for us, and conferred so many blessings upon us, and will do so in time to come, *let every creature in heaven, and on earth, and in the sea* and all depths *give praise, glory, honour, and blessing* to God. For He is our strength and our might, He alone is good, He alone is Most High, Almighty and wonderful, glorious and all-holy, to be praised and blessed to endless ages of ages. Amen.

(A WARNING TO THE WORLDLY)

But woe to the impenitent and to those who do not receive the Body and Blood of our Lord Jesus Christ, but indulge in wickedness and vice, pursuing evil passions and unholy desires. Woe to those who do not keep their promises, who surrender their bodies as slaves of the world, of carnal desires, and of the cares and pleasures of this world. Woe to those who at heart serve the devil and are deceived by him whose sons they are and whose will they do, for these are blind and cannot see the true light, our Lord Jesus Christ. They are destitute of spiritual wisdom, because the Son of God, the true Wisdom of the Father, does not dwell in them. It is said of them, *Their own wisdom is forgotten.* They see, know and do evil, and deliberately throw away their souls. Blind creatures that you are, led astray by your enemies the world, the flesh, and the devil! See how pleasant the body finds sin, and how distasteful the service of God! For, as the Gospel says, *It is from the heart of man that his wicked designs come.* Never will you possess any good, in this world or the next. You imagine that you have plenty of time in which to enjoy the vanities of this world, but you are mistaken, for the day and hour is approaching of which you refuse to think and prefer to remain in ignorance.

(THE TRAGEDY OF AN IMPENITENT DEATH)

The body falls sick, and death draws near; meanwhile relatives and friends gather, saying, 'Make your will.' The sick man's wife and children, relatives and friends, pretend to be sorry, and as he looks at them he is moved to ill-inspired emotion, thinking to himself, 'Now I place my soul, body, and all my possessions in your hands.' But lost indeed is the man who entrusts his soul and body into such hands, for the Lord says by His prophet, *Cursed shall he be that puts his trust in man.* Then they send for a priest, who says, 'Are you ready to do penance for all your sins?' He replies, 'I am.' 'Are you willing to make restitution from your property for the frauds and deceits that you have practised on others, so far as this is possible?' 'No,' he answers. 'Why not?' asks the priest. 'Because I have already disposed of all my property in favour of my relations and friends.' Then the wretched man begins to lose his power of speech, and is overtaken by a bitter death. Let all realize that whenever or however a person dies in his sins and without any attempt to make amends when he was able to do so, the devil tears his soul from his body with such agony and sorrow as is unexpressible save by one who has experienced it. All the talents, influence, knowledge, and wisdom that he thought were his are stripped from him. His relatives and friends seize upon his property and divide it, saying afterwards, 'Curse his soul! Why could he not have been more wealthy, and left us more!' Meanwhile the worms are feasting on his flesh. Thus during this brief life a man can lose both soul and body, and pass into hell, where he will suffer eternal torment.

In the name of the Father, and of the Son, and of the Holy Spirit. Amen. I, Brother Francis, desiring to kiss your feet, beg and implore you to welcome the fragrant words of our Lord Jesus Christ humbly and lovingly, to execute them gladly, and to obey them perfectly. Those who cannot read should have these words read to them frequently, and bear them in mind by putting them into practice until their lives' end, for *they are spirit and life*. Those who fail to do so will give an account at the Last Day before the judgement-seat of Christ. And may the Father, the Son, and the Holy Spirit bless all who gladly welcome the words of Christ, understand them, teaching others

to follow them by their own example, and persevering in them
to the end. Amen.

A LETTER SENT TOWARDS THE END OF HIS LIFE
TO THE CHAPTER GENERAL AND ALL THE FRIARS

*This letter to the Chapter General was sent shortly before Saint
Francis's death. Its tone and contents betray his anxiety about the
tendency to relax the high ideals of the primitive Rule and about the
worldliness of certain priests in the Order. He renews his promise to
keep the Rule in all its vigour, and states bluntly that those who are
not willing to be loyal to the ideals of the Order 'are not Catholics or
friars of mine.' He deals at length with the dignity and obligations of
the priestly office, and begs the Minister General and his successors to
maintain the discipline and ideals of the Order without equivocation.*

*IN the Name of the sublime Trinity and of the sacred Unity, the
Father, the Son, and the Holy Spirit. Amen.*

To all his revered and much loved brothers, to his superior the
Minister General of the Order of Minors and the Ministers
General who shall succeed him, to all Ministers, Guardians, and
humble priests of his Fraternity in Christ, and to all simple and
obedient friars, both long professed and newly admitted: I,
Brother Francis, a wretched and fallen man, your little servant,
send you greeting in the Name of Christ, Who has redeemed
and cleansed us in His Precious Blood. When you hear His
Name adore Him with fear and reverence, and cast yourselves
to the ground, for the Lord Jesus Christ, Son of the Most High,
is the Name of *Him Who is blessed for evermore. Amen.*

Hear my words, sons of the Lord and my brothers. Open *the
ears of your heart,* and obey the voice of the Son of God. Keep
His commandments with all your heart, and observe His

counsels with a perfect mind. *Give thanks unto the Lord for His goodness*, and glorify Him by your deeds, for He has sent you out into the whole world to testify to Him in word and deed, and to proclaim to all men that none is omnipotent but He. Persevere in discipline and in holy obedience. Keep your vows made to Him fully and faithfully. The Lord God offers Himself to you as to His children.

My brothers, I kiss your feet, and beg you with all my affection to show all possible reverence and honour to the most holy Body and Blood of our Lord Jesus Christ, *through Whom all things in heaven and on earth have been won back into union and peace with Almighty God.*

In the Name of the Lord I also beg all my friars who are, shall be, or hope to become priests of the Most High, to purify their hearts whenever they purpose to celebrate Mass, so as to offer the true sacrifice of the most holy Body and Blood of our Lord Jesus Christ reverently and with a pure and holy intention, not for any worldly motive, or out of fear or love for anyone, in order to please men. But with the help of God's grace let them direct their whole intention to the supreme Lord alone, desiring only to please Him Who acts in this Sacrament as He wills; for He says, *Do this for a commemoration of Me.* If any man does otherwise he becomes a traitor like Judas, and *will be held to account for the Lord's Body and Blood.*

Remember, my brothers who are priests, what is written in the Law of Moses, for those who transgressed it even in outward observance *died without mercy* in accordance with God's decree. And what of the man who has trampled the Son of God underfoot, who has reckoned the blood of the covenant, the very blood which sanctified him, as a thing unclean, and mocked at the Spirit that brought him grace? For, as the Apostle says, when a man does not distinguish or discern between the Holy Bread of Christ and other food, or when he *eats unworthily*, or when, although in a state of grace, he receives It carelessly and in vain, he despises, desecrates, and *tramples on* the Lamb of God. For

God says through His prophet, *Cursed is the man that doeth the work of God deceitfully.* And He denounces priests who refuse to lay this to heart, saying, *Falls my curse on all your blessings.*

Listen, my brothers. If the Blessed Virgin Mary is rightly honoured because she bore Christ in her most holy womb; if blessed John the Baptist trembled and was afraid to rest his hand on the head of the Holy One of God; if the tomb in which He rested awhile is held in veneration; how much more holy, righteous, and worthy should be the man who takes in his hands, receives into his mouth and heart, and administers to others the Lord Christ, no longer mortal but glorified, eternal and victorious, *on Whom the angels desire to satisfy their gaze.*

Consider your dignity, my brothers who are priests, and be holy, because He is holy. And since the Lord God has honoured you above all men through this holy Mystery, it is for you to love, reverence, and honour Him more than all men. It is a sad mistake and grave fault to be thinking of anything worldly when you have Him so close to you. Let mankind tremble, let the whole world shake, and the heavens rejoice when Jesus Christ, Son of the living God, descends to the altar in the hands of His priest! Oh, how wonderful is His dignity, and how amazing His condescension! Oh, humble sublimity! Oh, sublime humility, when the Lord of the universe, God and the Son of God, so humbles Himself as to conceal Himself beneath the simple form of bread for our salvation! Acknowledge the humility of God, my brothers, and *lay the homage of your hearts at His feet*; humble yourselves, so that He may exalt you. Withhold no part of yourselves from Him, so that He Who has given Himself so completely to you may Himself take full possession of you.

I counsel you in the Lord's Name that wherever the friars have houses only one Mass is to be said each day, and this is to be celebrated according to the use of Holy Church. If there are several priests in the house, let one be content to assist at the

189

Mass of another priest with love and charity, for our Lord grants equal grace to all who are worthy, both present and absent. For although our Lord may be found in many places, He remains entire and undiminished, and is One and the same everywhere, working as He pleases with the Lord God the Father, and the Holy Spirit the Paraclete throughout all ages. Amen.

And because *the man who belongs to God listens to God's words*, we have an especial obligation as regards the Divine Office, and must not only hear and obey the word of God, but reverently preserve both the (sacred) vessels and all books that contain His holy words, for in so doing we shall come to realize the sublime dignity of our Creator and the service that we owe Him. In His Name, therefore, I urge all my friars to treat the written words of God with all possible reverence wherever they may find them; and should it seem to them that they are not properly looked after or left lying about neglected, they are to collect them and put them in a fitting place, for in so doing they will honour the Lord Who spoke them. For many things are hallowed by the word of God, and it is by the merit of Christ's words that the Sacrament of the Altar is consecrated.

For myself, I confess all my sins before God the Father, the Son, and the Holy Spirit, to blessed Mary ever-virgin, to all the Saints in heaven and on earth, to the Minister-General of our Order as my revered superior, to all the priests of our Order, and to all my other blessed friars. I have offended in many matters by my own grievous fault, in particular because I have failed to observe the Rule which I have vowed to our Lord, and because of carelessness, sickness, ignorance or stupidity I have failed to recite the Office as the Rule requires.

I request my superior the Minister-General to ensure that all friars observe the Rule without violation, and that the clergy recite the Office before God devoutly. Their concern is not to produce vocal harmonies, but harmony of soul, so that the voice is at one with the soul, and the soul with God. In this way they will please God by their purity of soul, and will not be striving to please the ears of the people by the quality of their chanting.

God granting me grace, I strictly promise to observe these things myself, and shall trust the friars with me to fulfil their obligations regarding the Divine Office and other duties prescribed by the Rule. But if any of the brethren are unwilling to observe them, I do not regard them as Catholics or as friars of mine, and do not wish to see them or speak to them until they have done penance. I say the same of all others who wander about as they please and reject the discipline of the Rule, for our Lord Jesus Christ gave His life in order that He might not be lacking in obedience to His most holy Father. I, Brother Francis, the useless and unworthy creature of the Lord God, request Brother Elias, Minister-General of our whole Order, together with all Ministers-General who shall succeed him, and all Custodians and Guardians of the friars, both present and to come, to keep this letter of mine with them, to bear it in mind, and to follow its counsels. I beg them to take pains to observe all that is written in it, and cause it to be diligently followed in accordance with the pleasure of Almighty God now and always, so long as this world shall remain.

May God bless you who do these things, and may the Lord abide with you for ever.

ALMIGHTY, eternal, just, and merciful God, grant us miserable sinners grace that we may always do what we know to be Thy will, and always will as Thou willest; that inwardly cleansed, illumined, and kindled by the fire of the Holy Spirit, we may be enabled to follow in the footsteps of Thy Son our Lord Jesus Christ, and through Thy grace alone come to possess Thee, O Most High, Who livest and reignest in glory, perfect Trinity and undivided Unity, God Almighty, throughout all ages. *Amen.*

LETTER 3

TO A MINISTER

The un-named Minister to whom this letter is addressed is commonly thought to be Brother Elias, who became Minister in 1221. The letter appeals for love, tolerance, and restraint towards those who oppose him.

To our Brother Minister: the Lord bless you.

I give you my advice on the health of your soul and on the things that hinder your love of the Lord God to the best of my ability. If any friars or other people distress you or even strike you, regard these things as a means of grace. So be content with matters as they are, and do not seek to have them otherwise. You can attain this state of mind by true obedience to the Lord God and to me, for I am quite sure that this is the truest form of obedience. Love those who do you wrong, and hope for nothing from them but what the Lord shall grant you. Show your love for them by praying that they may become better Christians. This will bring greater benefit to your soul than living in a hermitage. On this point I would have you know that if you love the Lord and me His servant, you will show it in these ways: if some brother who has sinned, however gravely, come to you and asks pardon, never allow him to go away without receiving it. Even if he does not ask pardon, inquire whether he would not like to receive it. And if subsequently he comes to you a thousand times, love him more than you love me, and always show compassion on him so as to draw him to our Lord. And when you can do so, tell the Guardians that you are fully determined to act in this way.

With regard to all the articles in the Rule dealing with mortal sins, at the Whitsun Chapter with God's help and the advice of the brethren we will draw up a single article on these lines: If at the instigation of the devil any friar shall commit mortal sin, he shall be bound under obedience to appear before his Guardian.

The friars who know of his offence are not to abuse or disgrace him, but show great compassion to him and keep the sin of their brother concealed; for *it is not those who are in health that have need of the physician, it is those who are sick.* It is their duty under obedience to send him with a companion to his Guardian, and the Guardian is to deal mercifully with him, as he would wish to be treated were he in the same position.

If a friar commits any venial sin, he is to confess it to one of the brethren who is a priest; if no priest is available, let him confess to another friar until such time as he finds a priest to absolve him canonically, as already mentioned (*Rule I, Cap.* 20). Confessors have no authority to impose any other penance than this: *Go, and sin no more.*

In order to digest these matters the better, keep this letter with you until Whitsun when you will be attending Chapter with your brethren. And with the help of God apply yourself to work out these and any other points in the Rule that are not sufficiently clear.

LETTER 4

TO RULERS OF THE PEOPLE

Here the Saint appeals to those in high places not to allow their responsibilities to crowd out their religious obligations. Their position gives them opportunities to give a lead in devotion to their people, especially by their attendance at Mass.

To all princes and rulers, judges and governors throughout the world, and to all whom this letter shall reach: Brother Francis, your unworthy little servant in the Lord God, wishes you salvation and peace.

Bear in mind and realize that the day of our death is approaching. So I implore you most respectfully not to forget God or to fall away from His commandments because of your cares and worldly responsibilities; for *God's curse lies on all who swerve from His covenant,* and He will put them from His mind. When the hour of death comes they will lose everything that they thought their own; and the more learned and powerful they were in this world, the greater will be their suffering in hell.

My Lords, I earnestly urge you to set aside all worry and anxiety, and lovingly receive the most holy Body and Blood of our Lord Jesus Christ in remembrance of Him. See to it that all the people in your charge pay great honour to God. Let a time be set apart every evening and proclaimed by a herald or some other signal, when all the people offer praise and thanks to Almighty God. If you do not do this, remember that you will have to give an account before your Lord and God Jesus Christ at the Day of Judgement. May the Lord God bless all who keep a copy of this letter on their person and observe its counsels.

LETTER 5

TO ALL THE GUARDIANS OF THE FRIARS

This letter, addressed to the Guardians or superiors of all houses of the Order, asks them to use their influence to foster reverence for the Blessed Sacrament, especially among the secular clergy. The Saint emphasizes the need for penance and for the grace of the Sacraments.

To all Guardians of the Friars Minor who shall receive this letter, Brother Francis, your little servant in the Lord God, sends his greeting, wishing to call to your minds the new signs in heaven and earth which are mighty and noble in the sight of God but little understood by many Religious and other people.

Whenever you think it desirable or necessary, I beg you—not for my sake alone—to urge the clergy with all humility to give all possible reverence to the most holy Body and Blood of our

Lord Jesus Christ, to His holy Name, and to His recorded words by which the consecration of His Body is effected. Remind them to treat as sacred all chalices, corporals, ornaments of the altar, and everything that concerns the Holy Sacrifice. And should they ever find the most holy Body of our Lord unworthily housed, let them replace It and reserve It in a costly place with great honour as the laws of the Church require, and let them administer It to the people in a fitting manner. And whenever they discover the written words of our Lord lying about in neglected places they should gather them together and lay them in some suitable place.

In all your preaching urge the people to do penance, and tell them how none can be saved unless they receive the Body and Blood of our Lord. And when the Host is consecrated at the altar by the priest and carried from it, let all the people kneel and give praise, glory, and honour to the living and true Lord God.

It is my wish that all my brethren who are Guardians and receive this letter should keep this letter by them, and give copies to the other friars. And those who hold office as preachers or as Guardians of the friars are to have copies made, and to publish everything contained in this letter to the end. In so doing, let them know that they enjoy God's blessing and my own. And let these words of mine be binding on them under true and holy obedience.

LETTER 6

TO THE CLERGY

ON REVERENCE FOR THE BODY OF CHRIST AND THE CLEANLINESS OF THE ALTAR

Saint Francis's ardent devotion to the Blessed Sacrament here moves him to appeal to all priests to ensure that the holy mysteries are

celebrated fittingly even in the poorest churches, and the Sacrament
reserved in 'precious places.' It will be remembered that he took a lead
by sweeping out neglected churches, gathering up scattered books, and
providing altar vessels and wafers for Mass. This letter was probably
intended to be copied and circulated by the friars as they travelled
around the Provinces.

As clergy we must all be aware of the grave sin and ignorance
of which some are guilty regarding the most holy Body and
Blood of our Lord Jesus Christ and His most holy Name and
words by which His Body is consecrated. We know that His
Body cannot be present unless it is first hallowed by His own
word. For in this world we neither possess nor see anything of
the Most High Himself save His Body and Blood, His Name,
and His words, by which we have been created and redeemed
from death to life.

Therefore all who minister at such supremely sacred Mysteries
should take thought—especially those who minister carelessly—
how unworthy are the chalices, corporals, and linen used when
the Body and Blood of our Lord Jesus Christ is offered in
sacrifice. Many clergy reserve It in unworthy places; It is borne
on the roads without honour, received unworthily, and carelessly administered. The written Name and words of God are
sometimes trampled underfoot, for the natural man does not
discern the things of God. Shall we not be moved to reverence
in these matters, when our gracious Lord entrusts Himself to our
hands, and when we handle Him and daily receive Him into our
mouths? Do we not understand that it is we who should
entrust ourselves into His hands?

We must make swift and definite amends in all these faults,
and whenever the most holy Body and Blood of our Lord Jesus
Christ has been treated without honour or unfittingly reserved,
let it be removed and enshrined in a costly place. In the same
way, if the written Names and words of God are found lying in
neglected places, let them be collected together and laid in a

fitting place. We are well aware that it is our duty to observe these matters in obedience to the teachings of our Lord and the precepts of our Holy Mother the Church. And whosoever fails to observe these things, let him know that he will have to give account at the Day of Judgement. And be it known that whoever proclaims what I have written and secures its better observance shall receive the blessing of God.

LETTER 7

TO BROTHER LEO

Saint Francis writes to his beloved companion who is troubled by the tendency among new-comers in the Order to relax the Rule, and gives him permission to approach him directly for comfort and advice at any time.

BROTHER Leo, your brother Francis wishes you salvation and peace.

My son, I am writing to you as a mother, and in this letter I will remind you briefly of the advice that I gave you about all the matters that we discussed on our journey. If in due course you find it necessary to come and consult me, this is what I say: With the blessing of God and in obedience to me choose whatever way seems best to you and most pleasing to our Lord God in which to follow in the footsteps and poverty of Christ. And if you have need to come to me for the good of your soul or in order to receive some other consolation, and you wish to do so, then come, Leo.

A FRAGMENT OF THE RULE WRITTEN BY SAINT FRANCIS FOR THE SISTERS OF SAINT CLARE

SINCE God has inspired you to become daughters and servants of the most high and supreme King, our heavenly Father, and spouses of the Holy Spirit by electing to live in accordance with the perfection of the Gospel, I desire and promise on my part and that of my friars that I will always have a diligent care and especial concern for you as well as for them.

THE LAST WISH OF SAINT FRANCIS, WRITTEN BY HIM TO SAINT CLARE

I, LITTLE Brother Francis, desire to imitate the life and poverty of our most high Lord Jesus Christ and His most holy Mother, and to continue in it to the end. And I beg you, my ladies, and counsel you always to persevere in this most holy life and poverty. Take great care not to depart from it in any way because of any contrary teaching or advice from any source whatsoever.

LETTER 9

INSTRUCTIONS TO FRIARS LIVING IN A HERMITAGE

Saint Francis himself had felt a strong attraction to the life of a hermit, devoted to prayer and contemplation, and although, on the advice of Sister Clare and Brother Sylvester, he chose the harder role of public evangelist, he had every sympathy with those who retired to observe the Rule in all its austerity among the fastnesses of the moun-

tains. In this letter he advises those called to this way of life to live in very small 'families,' and lays down some broad principles to guide them.

THOSE friars who wish to lead the Religious Life in a hermitage should not number more than three or four at most. Two of them should act as mothers and two as sons, or one at least. Let the mothers lead the life of Mary and the sons the life of Martha.

Those who are leading the life of Mary should each have his own enclosure and cell, so that they do not have to live or sleep together. Compline should always be said at sunset, and the friars must be careful to observe silence, say their Hours, and rise at Matins. And let them *seek first the kingdom of God and His justice*. They should say Prime and Terce, and after Terce they may break silence to talk with their mothers. And whenever they so desire they may go out and ask alms for the love of God like other humble poor folk. Later in the day they should say Sext, None, and Vespers at the appointed times.

No one must be allowed to enter or eat in the enclosure where they live. The friars who act as mothers are to take care to remain in seclusion, and to keep their sons under obedience to avoid conversation with outsiders, so that no one can speak to them. The sons are not to talk to anyone but their own mothers, and to their Guardian whenever with God's blessing he sees fit to visit them. Let the sons exchange duties with the mothers from time to time by mutual consent. And let the friars be careful to observe these instructions carefully and diligently.

THE TESTAMENT OF SAINT FRANCIS

This is one of the most important and moving of Saint Francis's writings, composed after he had resigned the office of Minister-General. He speaks as founder and adviser of an Order that had grown beyond all his imagining and beyond his own control, and was swiftly diverging from his first ideals. His Testament is a last personal challenge and appeal to the brethren to return to these first ideals, especially of poverty, simplicity, and obedience. He speaks simply of his own conversion, his faith in the Church and Sacraments. He tells of the early days of the brotherhood, and his conviction that they 'must live according to the teachings of the Gospels.' He forbids the friars to accumulate property and privileges like the older monastic Orders, and exalts the virtue of obedience to authority within the Order. Finally, knowing that the main danger to his ideals springs from worldly-mindedness and ambition among the Ministers, he directs them to read this Testament at every Chapter, and forbids them under obedience to water down the plain meaning of his words by any private interpretations of their own.

THE Lord granted me, Brother Francis, grace to begin to do penance, for while I was living in sin, it seemed a very bitter thing to look at lepers; but the Lord Himself led me among them, and I had compassion on them. And when I left them, the thing that had seemed so horrible to me was transformed into happiness of body and soul for me. After this I delayed awhile, and then renounced the world. And the Lord gave me such faith in His Church that I prayed to Him in simplicity and said, 'We adore Thee, O Lord Jesus Christ, here and in all Thy churches throughout the world, and we bless Thee, for by Thy holy Cross Thou hast redeemed the world.'

After this the Lord gave me, and still gives me, such faith in priests who live according to the precepts of the holy Roman Church in respect of their Orders, that even were they to persecute me, I would wish to resort to them. And had I the great wisdom of Solomon, and found very poor secular priests, I would not preach in their parishes without their consent. I wish to respect them and all others, and to love and honour them as my masters; and I will not see any sin in them, because I see the Son of God in them, and look on them as my masters. And I wish the most holy Sacrament to be honoured above all things, and venerated in places of honour. And wherever I find writings bearing God's most holy Name and Word lying in unfitting places, I gather them together and put them in a worthy place. And we should honour and respect all theologians, and those who teach the most holy Word of God as those who minister spirit and life to us.

After the Lord had given me brethren, no man showed me what to do; but the Most High Himself revealed to me how I must live according to the teachings of the Holy Gospel. And I dictated a simple Rule in a few words, and the Lord Pope confirmed it for me. And those who came to embrace this way of life gave all that they possessed to the poor, and were content with a single habit, patched inside and out, and a cord and breeches. And we had no desire for anything more.

Those of us who were in Orders recited the Office like other clergy, while the lay-brethren said the *Our Father*. And we were content to live in abandoned churches, and to be looked on as ignorant and inferior to all men. I myself work with my hands, and wish to do so; and it is my firm intention that all other friars should work in some honest occupation. Those who do not know a craft must learn, not in order to make a profit from their labour, but to set a good example and avoid idleness. And whenever we are not given our due wages for work, let us approach the Lord's table and seek alms from door to door.

The Lord has revealed to me that we should use this greeting,

'The Lord give you peace.' Let all the brethren beware of accepting churches, houses, or anything provided for them unless they conform to Holy Poverty, to which we are vowed in our Rule, always lodging *as strangers and exiles*.

I strictly forbid all friars under holy obedience, wherever they may be, to presume to solicit any letters (*of privilege*) from the Roman Curia, either in person or indirectly, whether it be for a church or other place, under the pretext that it is necessary for preaching or to avoid persecution. Wherever they are not welcome, let them go to another place and do penance with the blessing of God.

For myself, I firmly purpose to obey the Minister-General of this Fraternity and any Guardian whom he is pleased to appoint over me. I am content to be entirely in his hands, so that I cannot go anywhere or do anything contrary to obedience and to his will. At the same time, I wish always to have a priest to minister to me as is enjoined in the Rule.

Let all the other friars be obliged to obey their Guardians, and to fulfil their obligations under the Rule. And should it be found that anyone does not fulfil his obligations according to the Rule and wishes to deviate from it, or is not a good Catholic, then all his other brethren, wherever they may be, are required under obedience to bring him before the nearest Guardian. The Guardian is to keep him confined like a prisoner day and night, so that he cannot escape from custody until he hands him over personally to his own Minister. And the Minister is likewise required under obedience to keep him in charge of suitable brethren, who are to watch him day and night until they can bring him before the Lord Cardinal of Ostia, who is the master, Protector, and corrector of this Fraternity.

The brethren are not to say, 'This is a new Rule,' for it is a reminder, a warning, and an encouragement. It is my Testament which I, little Brother Francis, make for you, my blessed brothers, with the intention that as Catholics we may better obey the Rule which we have promised our Lord to obey.

The Minister-General and all other Ministers and Guardians are bound under obedience not to add or subtract anything from these words of mine. They are to keep this Testament always with them, together with the Rule, and at every Chapter which they summon, when they read the Rule, let them read these words as well.

I strictly enjoin all my brethren, both clergy and lay-brothers, under obedience not to add glosses to the Rule or to my words, saying, 'It shall be understood thus.' But as our Lord has granted me to speak simply and clearly, so shall you understand them simply and clearly, and observe them with holy deeds until the end.

Whosoever observes these things shall be filled with the blessing of our most high Father in heaven, and on earth he shall be blessed by His beloved Son, by the Holy Spirit the Paraclete, by all the powers of heaven, and by all the Saints.

And I, Brother Francis, your little servant, to the utmost of my power, confirm you inwardly and outwardly in this most holy blessing. *Amen.*

THE FIRST RULE OF THE FRIARS MINOR

Saint Francis had the temperament of an artist and a poet, and had little taste for rules and regulations, wishing only to follow Christ simply and sincerely in the spirit of the Gospels. At first he probably did not envisage the swift growth of his little brotherhood into a great Order, but he was quick to read the signs of the times, and realized that if his friars were to fulfil a useful purpose, they must obtain the blessing and guidance of the Church on their life and work. Accordingly in 1210, when his brethren reached the apostolic number of twelve, Saint Francis wrote a simple Rule and set out for Rome to obtain the approval of the Pope.

Innocent III himself was deeply aware of the need for a spiritual revolution within the Church, but had been sorely tried by well-meaning but misguided reformers whose activities had resulted in harmful heresies and schisms. Despite his natural caution he therefore gave Saint Francis a careful hearing, and when the latter put aside the Pope's suggestion that he should join one of the established Orders and continued to plead for permission to observe the precepts of the Gospel in absolute poverty and simplicity, he yielded to his urgency and gave verbal approval to his Rule, but reserved a more formal decision on the matter until this new type of religious fraternity had proved itself.

The rapid growth of the Order, its organization into Provinces, and the appointment of Cardinal Ugolino as Protector brought great changes, many of them distasteful to Saint Francis. On his return from the Holy Land in the summer of 1220 he found the Order rent with dissension between those who wished the Order to conform to traditional lines, with houses, property, and schools, and those who clung to his ideal of primitive simplicity and absolute poverty. Feeling that he no longer enjoyed the support of the majority, Saint Francis resigned his office as Minister-General to Peter Catanii, and retired to S. Mary of the Angels to revise the Rule, of which Father Cuthbert says: 'It *was not a treaty of peace; it was a challenge thrown down to those who would change the vocation of the Fraternity; and as such it was taken by the dissident Ministers.'* In it *he restates his prohibition against the ownership of property, and the ideal of absolute poverty and simplicity.*

It is uncertain whether the Chapter of the Order approved the Rule, but it did not receive papal sanction and therefore remained inoperative. It failed to satisfy either Saint Francis or the Ministers.

IN THE NAME OF THE FATHER, AND OF THE SON, AND OF THE HOLY SPIRIT. AMEN.

THIS is the Rule of life which blessed Francis petitioned the Holy Father Innocent to grant and approve. And the Holy Father granted and approved it for him and his friars, present and to come.

Brother Francis and all who succeed him as Head of this Order promise obedience and respect to the Holy Father Innocent and his successors. And all other friars shall be bound to obey Brother Francis and his successors.

1

That the friars shall live in obedience and chastity, without worldly possessions.

THE Rule and way of life of our brethren is this: to live under obedience, in chastity, and without possessions, and to follow the teaching and footsteps of our Lord Jesus Christ, Who said:

'*If thou hast a mind to be perfect, go home and sell all that belongs to thee; give it to the poor, and so the treasure thou hast shall be in heaven; then come back and follow Me.*'

'*If any man has a mind to come My way, let him renounce self, and take up his cross, and follow Me.*'

'*If any man comes to Me, without hating his father and mother and wife and children and brethren and sisters, yes, and his own life too, he can be no disciple of Mine.*'

'*Every man that has forsaken home, or brothers, or sisters, or father, or mother, or wife, or children, or lands for My Name's sake, shall receive his reward a hundredfold, and obtain everlasting life.*'

2

On the admission of friars, and their clothing.

IF any man is inspired by God to adopt this way of life and comes to our brethren, he is to be kindly received. If he perseveres in his wish to follow our way of life, the friars shall take care not to interfere with his worldly affairs, but shall bring him to their Minister as soon as possible. The Minister is to receive him with kindness, give him encouragement, and carefully explain to him our life. After this, if the postulant so desires and can do so without any spiritual obstacle, let him arrange to dispose of all his property and distribute it among the poor. But the friars and Ministers of the friars must carefully avoid any interference with his arrangements, and must neither receive any money or benefit from it through a third person. But if they are in need, the friars may accept bodily necessities like other poor people, provided they do not accept money. When the postulant has returned, the Minister is to give him the habit of probation for one year, and this is to consist of two habits without the hood, a cord, breeches, and a waist-length cloak. When the year's probation has been completed, the Minister may accept his vow of obedience. After this the new brother will not be allowed to join another Order or to excuse himself from obedience, in accordance with the decree of the Lord Pope. For the Gospel says, *No one who looks behind him, when he has*

once put his hand to the plough, is fitted for the Kingdom of God.
But if a man comes to us who cannot dispose of his property
because of family responsibilities, although he has the will to do
so, let him relinquish control of it and this shall suffice.

The other friars who have made vows of obedience shall have
a single habit with a hood, and if necessary another without it,
together with a cord and breeches. All friars are to be clothed
in poor garments, and may patch them with sackcloth and other
pieces with God's blessing, for our Lord says in the Gospel, *You
must look in kings' palaces for men that go proudly dressed and live in
luxury.* Even if they are abused as hypocrites they are not to
cease doing good. And they are not to aspire to costly robes in
this world, so that they may receive the robes of the Kingdom
of Heaven.

3

On the Divine Office and on fasting.

OUR Lord says, *This kind of devil cannot be cast out except by
prayer and fasting.* And, *When you fast, do not be gloomy like
hypocrites.* So all friars, both clergy and lay-brothers, are to
recite the Divine Office, Praises, and prayers according to the
appointed use. Clergy will say the office for the living and
the dead as other clergy do. Every day they will recite the
Miserere mei, Deus and the *Paternoster* in reparation for the
omissions and negligence of the brethren, and they are to say
the *De profundis* and the *Paternoster* for departed brethren. They
may only possess such books as are essential to the performance
of their office. Lay brothers who can read may have a psalter,
but others who cannot read may not have books. The lay
brothers shall say the *Credo* and twenty-four *Paternosters* and
Glorias for Matins and five for Lauds; the *Credo* and seven
Paternosters with the *Gloria* for Prime; seven of each for Terce,
Sext, and None; twelve for Vespers; and the *Credo* with seven

Paternosters and *Glorias* for Compline. They are also to say seven *Paternosters* and the *Requiem aeternam* for the departed, and three *Paternosters* daily in reparation for the omissions and negligences of the brethren.

Similarly, all friars are to fast from the feast of All Saints until the Nativity of our Lord, and from Epiphany—the time when our Lord began His fast—until Easter. This Rule imposes no other obligation to fast except on Fridays. And they are allowed to eat any food that is set before them, as the Gospel teaches.

4

On the Ministers and their authority over other friars.

IN the Lord's Name, let all friars who are appointed Ministers and servants of the others assemble the brethren in their own provinces and houses, and let them pay frequent visits to give them spiritual counsel and encouragement. Let all my other blessed brethren render them due obedience in all matters that concern the salvation of their souls and are not contrary to the Rule. Let them act towards one another as our Lord commands: *Do to other men all that you would have them do to you*, and, do nothing to others that you would not wish to be done to yourself. The Ministers and servants of the brethren are to remember our Lord's words, *I did not come to have service done to Me, but to serve others*. The souls of the friars have been entrusted to their care, and if a single one of them is lost through their ill doing or bad example, they will have to render account before our Lord Jesus Christ at the Day of Judgement.

5

On the correction of faults in the friars.

GUARD your own souls and those of the brethren, for *it is a fearful thing to fall into the hands of the living God*. Should a

Minister give any friar an order contrary to our Rule or against his conscience, the friar is not obliged to obey him, for obedience is not enjoined when it involves committing a fault or sin. All brethren under obedience to the Ministers and servants are therefore to give careful and close attention to the behaviour of the Ministers themselves. And if one of them is seen to be acting in a worldly manner and not spiritually in accordance with the precepts of our Rule, and if after three warnings he does not amend, he is to be deposed from his office as Minister and servant of the whole brotherhood at the next Whitsun Chapter, however great the opposition may be. If any of the friars anywhere wants to live a worldly life and neglects the spiritual life, his brother friars are to warn and reprove him, trying to correct him diligently and humbly. But if after three warnings he refuses to mend his ways, his brethren are to report the matter to his own Minister and servant, or send him to him as soon as possible; and the Minister is to do with him whatever he thinks best in the eyes of God.

All friars, both Ministers and others, are to avoid giving way to anxiety or anger at the wrongdoing or bad example of another, for through one man's sin the devil tries to corrupt many others. They are to help the offender as well as they may by spiritual means, for *it is not those who are in health that have need of the physician, it is those who are sick.*

Friars are not to behave in a haughty and overbearing manner, especially among themselves, for our Lord says in the Gospel, *Among the Gentiles those who bear rule lord it over them, and great men vaunt their power over them.* But it shall not be so among the friars, for *whoever would be a great man among you must be your minister and servant, and whoever is great among you must become the least of all.*

No friar is to wrong or malign another; on the contrary, all are to serve and obey one another gladly in the spirit of charity. This is the true and holy obedience of our Lord Jesus Christ. Let all friars who fall away from God's commandments and revolt from obedience realize that so long as they deliberately persist in such wickedness they fall under the rebuke of the prophet, who said, *Thy curse lies on all who swerve from Thy covenant.* But so long as they adhere to the commandments of the Lord, as they have vowed to do by the Holy Gospel and by their Rule, they can rest assured that they are living in true obedience and enjoy the blessing of God.

6

On the friars' right of appeal to their Ministers; and that no brother is to be called Prior.

WHEREVER they may be, friars who find it impossible to observe our Rule of life are to visit their Minister and explain the circumstances to him. The Minister is to search carefully for such a solution as he would desire were he in their position. And no brother is to be called Prior, but all alike are to be known as Friars Minor. And let them all wash one another's feet.

7

On the forms of work and service suitable for the friars.

No friars, wherever they serve or work as employees of other men, are to be chamberlains, cellarers or stewards in the households of those whom they serve. They are not to accept any office that might cause scandal or do harm to their own souls. They are to occupy humble posts and be at the beck and call of all in the house.

Friars who know a trade are to work at it and use their former knowledge, provided that it is not contrary to the salvation of their souls and that they can put it to good use. For the prophet says, *Thyself shall eat what thy hands have toiled to win; blessed thou art; all good shall be thine.* And the Apostle Paul says, *Each of you is to remain, brethren, in the condition in which he was called.* And, *The man who refuses to work must be left to starve.* The friars may accept all necessities of life, but no money. And should it be necessary, let them go and beg alms like other brethren. And they may possess tools and gear necessary for their work.

Every friar is to keep occupied in useful work, for it is written, 'Always be occupied in some good work, so that the devil may not find you idle.' And again, 'Idleness is the enemy of the soul.' So the servants of God should always be employed, either in prayer or in some other worthy occupation.

Wherever friars may be, whether in hermitages or in other places, they are to beware of becoming owners of any property or of displacing other people. Whoever comes to them, whether friend or foe, thief or bandit, is to be given a kindly welcome. And wherever the brethren find themselves, they are to be careful to honour and respect one another devoutly and without complaint. Let the friars beware of appearing sad and gloomy, like hypocrites; let them show themselves gay and happy, and be pleasant to all.

8

That the friars may not accept money.

OUR Lord teaches in the Gospel, *Look well and keep yourselves clear of all malice and covetousness; and keep yourselves unentangled in worldly business and the cares of this life.* Therefore no friar, wherever he may be or go, shall ever take, accept, or cause to be accepted any money or coin, whether for the purchase of clothes or books or as payment for any work. He may only accept it in the case of obvious necessity on behalf of sick brethren, because we may not regard money as any more valuable than pebbles: the devil wishes to blind those who value it any higher. We who have renounced everything must beware of losing the Kingdom for so trifling a thing. And should we

211

happen to find money anywhere, we should esteem it no more than the dust that we trample underfoot, for it is *a shadow's shadow; a world of shadows.* Should any friar happen to pick up or keep money—which heaven forbid—excepting only for the needs of the sick as I have mentioned, all the brethren shall regard him as a false brother, a thief, a robber, and a receiver unless he sincerely repents. And on no account are friars to accept money as alms, to organize collections, or to accept money collected by others, either for a friary or any other building; nor are they to accompany anyone who is collecting money for such places. But with God's blessing the brethren may undertake all kinds of work that are not contrary to our Rule. In the case of absolute necessity, they may, however, ask alms for the support of lepers. But they must always have a great fear of money, and they must not travel around the countryside for the sake of base gain.

9

On asking for alms.

ALL friars are to set themselves to imitate the humility and poverty of our Lord Jesus Christ, and must remember that, in the words of the Apostle, we are to possess nothing in the whole world except food and clothing, and to be content with these. Let them be happy to associate with humble and insignificant people, the poor and the weak, the sick, the lepers, and the beggars on the roads. And whenever necessary, let them ask for alms. They are not to be ashamed, but remember that our Lord Jesus Christ, the Son of the living and Almighty God, set His face like a flint and was not ashamed, for both Christ Himself, the blessed Virgin, and His disciples were poor and strangers, and lived on alms. Whenever people abuse the friars and refuse to give them alms, let them thank God, for at the judgement seat of our Lord Jesus Christ they will receive honours in return

212

for their humiliations. Let them realize that these humiliations will not be blamed on those who suffer them, but on those who inflict them. Moreover, alms are a heritage and right due to the poor, a right won for us by our Lord Jesus Christ. Brethren who obtain alms by their labour shall receive a great reward, and shall win blessings for those who give them; for the goods that men leave behind them in this world will perish, but the charity and alms that they have given will earn a reward from the Lord.

Each friar is to make his wants known to his brother, so that he can obtain his needs. Let each cherish his brother as a mother loves and cherishes her child, for God will grant him grace to do this. And *let not one man, over his meat, mock at him who does not eat it, or the other, while he abstains, pass judgement on him who eats it.* And when necessary, all brethren everywhere are permitted to eat any kind of food that others eat, as our Lord said of David, *who ate the loaves set forth there before God, which only the priests may eat.* They are to remember Christ's words, *Look well to yourselves; do not let your hearts grow dull with revelry and drunkenness and the affairs of this life, so that that day overtakes you unawares; it will come like the springing of a trap on all those who dwell upon the face of the earth.* And in times of obvious need all the brethren are to satisfy their wants in whatever way the Lord shall direct them, for necessity knows no law.

10

On sick friars.

WHEN any brother falls sick, the others are not to leave him, wherever he may be, unless one or more of them have been appointed to look after him as they would wish to be cared for themselves. In an emergency they may entrust him to another person to look after him in his illness. And I ask any friar who is ill to give thanks to the Creator for all things; whether in sickness or in health he must learn to conform his own will to the will of God, for He moulds and trains all whom He has chosen for eternal life by the scourges of chastisement and sickness and by the grace of contrition, and has said, *It is those I love that I correct and chasten.* But if the sick brother is ill-tempered and complains against God and his brethren, or if he persistently demands medicines in his anxiety to restore his body—which is soon to perish and is an enemy of the soul—he shows himself to be prompted by the flesh and the devil and unworthy to be one of the brethren because he loves his body better than his soul.

11

That friars are not to swear or slander, but must love one another.

ALL friars are to be careful not to slander anyone or enter into quarrels; it is better for them to keep silence whenever God gives them grace to do so. They are not to dispute among themselves, but school themselves to reply humbly, *We are servants, and worthless.* And they are not to be angry, for *any man who is angry with his brother must answer for it before the court of justice, and any man who says Raca to his brother must answer for it before the Council; and any man who says to his brother, Thou fool, must answer for it in hell fire.* Therefore let the brethren love one another, for our Lord says, *This is My command, that you should love one another, as I have loved you.* They must show the love that they should feel in action, as the Apostle says, *Let us show our love by the true test of action, not by taking phrases on our lips.* They are not to speak evil of others, to grumble, or to disparage others, for the Scriptures say, *Slanderers and detractors are enemies of God.* But then be modest and gentle to all men. They are not to judge or condemn others, because God bids us not to consider the sins of others, but in bitterness of soul to recall our own. They are to *fight their way in at the narrow door,* for the

Lord says, *How small is the gate, how narrow the road, that leads on to life, and how few there are that find it.*

12

On immodest looks, and on avoiding the company of women.

WHEREVER they are, all friars are to avoid immodest looks and the company of women, and no brother is to converse with them alone. Priests may fittingly speak to them when giving penance or advice of any kind. And no friar shall be allowed to accept a vow of obedience from any woman, but once she has received spiritual counsel, the woman is to perform her penance wherever she desires. We must all keep watch over ourselves and maintain all our powers in purity, for the Lord says, *He who casts his eyes on a woman so as to lust after her has already committed adultery with her in his heart.*

13

On the punishment for fornication.

IF any friar is instigated by the devil to commit fornication, he shall be stripped of the habit of the Order, which he has forfeited by his scandalous conduct. He is to be deprived of all privileges and expelled from our Order. Afterwards, he is to do penance for his sins.

14

How friars are to travel about the world.

WHEN friars travel about the world they are to take nothing for their journey, *neither purse nor wallet, nor bread, nor money, nor a staff.* And whenever they enter a house, they shall first say,

'Peace be to this house.' And they are to remain in that house, *eating and drinking what they have to give them.* They are not to offer resistance to injury, but if anyone strikes them on one cheek, let them turn the other as well. If anyone takes away their habit, let them have their cloak as well. Let them give to everyone who asks, and if anyone takes away anything that is theirs, they must not try to recover it.

15

That friars may not own or ride beasts.

I FORBID all my friars, whether clergy or lay, whether they travel about or remain in their houses, to own any beast, or to have the use of other people's animals. They are not allowed to ride except in the case of infirmity or great necessity.

16

On friars who go among Saracens or other unbelievers.

OUR Lord says, *Remember, I am sending you out to be like sheep among wolves; you must be wary, then, as serpents and yet innocent as doves.* So those friars whom God inspires to go among the Saracens and other unbelievers may do so with the approval of their Minister and servant. The Minister is to grant permission and not oppose them, provided that he considers them suitable men to send, for if he acts unwisely in this or other matters he will have to give account to God. There are two ways in which the friars who go out can act with spiritual effect. The first is not to dispute or be contentious, but *for love of the Lord to bow to every kind of human authority,* and to acknowledge themselves Christians. The other way, whenever they think it to be God's will, is to proclaim the word of God and their faith in God Almighty, the Father, the Son, and the Holy Spirit, Creator of all things, showing that the Son is our Redeemer and Saviour, and teaching men that they must be baptized and become Christians, for *no man can enter into the Kingdom of God unless birth comes to him from water, and from the Holy Spirit.*

These truths and others acceptable to the Lord they must teach to others, for our Lord says in the Gospel, *Whoever acknowledges Me before men, I too will acknowledge him before My Father Who is in heaven,* and, *Whoever disowns Me and My words, the Son of Man will disown when He comes in the glory of the Father and of the holy angels.*

All friars everywhere are to remember that they have given and surrendered themselves soul and body to our Lord Jesus Christ, and for love of Him they must expose themselves to all enemies, both visible and invisible; for our Lord says, *The man who loses his life for My sake shall save it in life everlasting. Blessed are those who suffer persecution in the cause of right; the Kingdom of Heaven is theirs. They will persecute you just as they have persecuted Me. If they persecute you in one city, take refuge in another. Blessed are you when men hate and revile you, and when they cast you off and censure you, and reject your name as something evil, and speak all manner of evil against you falsely because of Me. When that day comes, rejoice and exult over it, for a rich reward awaits you in heaven. I tell you, My friends, there is no need to fear those who kill the body, but have no means of killing the soul. See to it that you are not disturbed in mind. It is by endurance that you will secure possession of your souls. The man will be saved who endures to the last.*

17

On preachers.

No friar is to preach contrary to the teachings and practices of the holy Roman Church, and none is to preach without the approval of his Minister. The Minister is to be careful not to grant permission to any friar without due thought. But let every friar make his own life a sermon to others. No Minister or preacher is to take upon himself the administration of the brethren or the office of preaching, and whenever he is called upon to do so, he must surrender his office without argument. *In love which is God* I beg all my brethren, whether preaching, praying or labouring, clergy and laymen alike, to do their utmost to be humble in all things. They are not to boast or flatter themselves, to take secret pleasure in their good words or deeds, or in any kind of good that God may speak or effect through them at any time. For our Lord says, *It is not for you to rejoice that the devils are made subject to you.*

Let us be sure that nothing is ours but our own faults and sins. Indeed, we should be glad when we are exposed to various temptations and undergo all kinds of hardship and trouble in soul or body in this world so that we may win eternal life. So let all the brethren beware of pride and vainglory. We must guard ourselves against the wisdom of the world and the prudence of the flesh, for these take a great delight in words but very little in deeds; the worldly man has no desire for true religion and inward holiness of soul, but wants his religion and piety to be seen by men. It is of such people that our Lord says, *Believe Me, they have their reward already.* But the spirit that belongs to God wishes the body to be mortified and despised, reviled and humiliated, and cultivates humility and patience, pure simplicity, and true peace of soul. Above all it desires the fear of the Lord, wisdom from above, and the divine love of the Father, the Son, and the Holy Spirit.

We must ascribe all good to the Lord God, most high and supreme, and acknowledge that all good proceeds from Him. Let us thank Him, the Author of all good things, for He is supreme and sublime, the only true God, Who alone may receive and accept all honour and reverence, all praise and blessing, all thanks and all glory. He alone is good, and from all good things do come. And whenever we see or hear evil said or done, or if we hear God blasphemed, let us bless Him, do good, and praise the Lord Who is blessed for evermore. *Amen.*

18

How Ministers are to hold meetings.

EACH year on the feast of Saint Michael the Archangel all Ministers are to assemble with their colleagues at whatever place they choose in order to confer together on the things of God. Once every three years, unless the Minister-General of the whole Order decides otherwise, all Ministers are to attend a Chapter at the Church of S. Mary of the Porziuncula. Those Ministers who live overseas or beyond the Alps are to attend every third year, and the remainder of the Ministers every year.

19

That the friars are to live as Catholics.

ALL friars shall be Catholics, and shall live and speak as Catholics. If any errs from the Catholic Faith and life by his words or actions, and refuses to amend his ways, he is to be expelled from our fraternity. In matters relating to the salvation of the soul and in all that is not contrary to our religion, we should regard all clergy and religious as our masters, and respect their order, their office, and their authority.

20

On the friars' confessions, and the reception of Holy Communion.

MY blessed brethren, clergy and lay alike, shall confess their sins to priests of our own Order. If this is impossible, they may confess to other discreet Catholic priests, in the sure knowledge and understanding that, provided that they humbly and faithfully perform the penance imposed on them, they are undoubtedly absolved from their sins irrespective of whatever priests give them penance and absolution. But if a priest is not to be found, they are to confess to one another, as the Apostle James prescribes: *Confess your sins to one another.* But if they do this, they must not omit to visit a priest afterwards, for priests alone have authority to bind and to loose.

When contrite and shriven, let the brethren receive the Body and Blood of our Lord Jesus Christ with great humility and reverence, mindful that our Lord said, *The man who eats My flesh and drinks My Blood enjoys eternal life,* and, *Do this for a commemoration of Me.*

21

The call to praise and penance that friars may deliver.

WITH the blessing of God all my friars may deliver this exhortation and call to praise before any assembly whenever they so desire: 'Fear and honour, praise and bless, thank and adore the Lord God Almighty, in Trinity and Unity, the Father, the Son, and the Holy Spirit, Creator of all things. Do penance, and produce worth-while results from your repentance, for you know that you must soon die. Be generous to others, and they will be generous to you. Forgive, and you shall be forgiven. If you do not forgive others their offences, the Lord will not forgive you your offences. Confess all your sins. Blessed are those who die in penitence, for they shall enter the Kingdom of Heaven. Woe to those who do not die in penitence, for they shall become the children of the devil who do his bidding and will go into eternal fire. Be prepared, guard yourselves from evil, and persevere in good to the end.'

22

An exhortation to friars.

My brothers, let us all obey the words of our Lord, *Love your enemies, and do good to those who hate you.* For our Lord Jesus Christ, in Whose footsteps we must follow, addressed His betrayer as a friend, and voluntarily surrendered Himself to those who crucified Him. Our friends, therefore, are all who unjustly inflict upon us trouble and distress, shame and injury, grief and pain, martyrdom and death, and we should feel great love for such people, because it is through these things that we win eternal life. And we should hate our own body with its vices and sins, because carnal living causes us to lose the love of our Lord Jesus Christ and eternal life and to be lost in hell; for our sins render us abhorrent, wretched and hardened against good, and eager and ready for evil. For our Lord says in the Gospel, *It is from man's heart that his wicked designs come, his sins of adultery, fornication, murder, robbery, greed, wickedness, deceit, lust, hatred, slander, blasphemy, pride, and folly. All these evils issue from the heart, and it is these that make a man unclean.*

But since we have renounced the world, our sole duty is to obey the will of our Lord and to please Him. We must beware of becoming like the stony or thorn-choked soil by the roadside spoken of by our Lord, Who said, *The seed is the word of God. That which fell by the roadside and was trampled upon represents those who hear the word of God and do not grasp it; and at once the evil one comes and carries off what was sown in their hearts, and takes away the word from their hearts lest they should believe and be saved. Those who took in the seed in rocky ground are those who hear the word and at once entertain it gladly; there is no root in them, and they do not last long, for no sooner does tribulation or persecution arise over the word than their faith is shaken. And those who took in the seed in the midst of briers are those who hear the word of God, but allow the cares of this world and the false charms of riches and other desires to enter and stifle the word, so that it remains fruitless. Whereas those who took in the seed in good soil are those who hear God's word, grasp and follow it with a good and sincere heart, and bear fruit with patience.*

My brothers, this is why we must do as our Lord says, and *leave the dead to bury their dead.* We must beware of the malice and cunning of Satan, who does not want any man to turn his heart and mind toward the Lord God. He roams around hoping to capture a man's heart by offering some illusory advantage or help, and thus to stifle God's word. He tries to obliterate the teachings and precepts of our Lord from his mind, to blind him with worldly business and anxieties, and to make his dwelling in him. For our Lord tells us, *The unclean spirit, which has possessed a man and then goes out of him, walks about the desert looking for a resting-place, and finds none; and it says, I will go back to my own dwelling, from which I came out. And it comes back, to find that dwelling empty, and swept out, and in order. Thereupon it goes away, and brings in seven other spirits more wicked than itself to bear it company, and together they enter in and settle down there; so that the last state of that man is worse than the first.*

So we must all be on our guard, my brothers, lest the illusion of gain, success or help should cause us to love other things and turn our minds and hearts away from God. But in the name of holy love, which is God, I beg all my friars, Ministers as well as others, to thrust every difficulty, care, and anxiety behind them, and to serve, love, worship, and honour the Lord God with all their strength, with a pure heart and mind, for this is what He desires above all things. We should at all times make a dwelling place within our hearts for Him Who is Lord God Almighty, the Father, the Son, and the Holy Spirit, Who has said, *Keep watch, then, praying at all times, so that you may be found worthy to come safe through all that lies before you, and stand erect in the presence of the Son of Man. And when you pray, say, Our Father, Who art in heaven.* Let us worship Him with a pure heart, because *we ought to pray continually, and never be discouraged, for such men as these the Father claims for His worshippers. God is a spirit, and those who worship Him must worship Him in spirit and in truth.* Let us turn to Him Who is *our Shepherd and keeps watch over our souls,* Who says, *I am the good Shepherd. I feed My sheep, and I lay down My life for My sheep. All of you are brothers. Call no man on earth your father; you have but one Father, and He is in heaven. And do not be called teachers, for Christ is your only Teacher, and He is in heaven. As long as you live on in Me, and My words live on in you, you will be able to make what request you will, and have it granted. Wherever two or three are gathered together in My Name, I am there in the midst of them. Now I am with you always until the consummation of the world. The words I have been speaking to you are spirit and life. I am the Way; I am Truth and Life.*

Let us hold firmly to the words, the life, the teaching, and the holy Gospel of Christ, Who deigned to pray for us to His Father and reveal His Name to us, saying, *Father, I have made Thy Name known to the men whom Thou hast entrusted to Me, and they, receiving it, recognized it for truth that I came from Thee, and found faith to believe that it was Thou Who didst send Me. It is for these I pray; I am not praying for the world, but for those whom Thou hast entrusted to Me; they belong to Thee, as all that I have is Thine, and all that Thou hast is Mine. Holy Father, keep them true to Thy name, Thy gift to Me, that they may be one, as we are one. While I am still in the world I am telling them this, so that My joy may be theirs. I have given them Thy message, and the world has nothing but hatred for them because they do not belong to the world, as I, too, do not belong to the world. I am not asking that Thou shouldst take them out of the world, that Thou shouldst keep them clear of what is evil. Keep them holy, then, through the truth; it is Thy word that is truth. Thou hast sent Me into the world on Thy errand, and I have sent them into the world on My errand. And I dedicate Myself for their sakes, that they too may be dedicated through the truth. It is not only for them that I pray; I pray for those who are to find faith in Me through their word; that they may all be one . . . so that the world may come to believe that it is Thou Who hast sent Me, and Thou hast bestowed Thy love upon them, as Thou hast bestowed it upon Me. This, Father, is My desire, that all those whom Thou hast entrusted to Me may be with Me where I am, so as to see Thy glory in Thy kingdom.*

23

Prayer, praise, and thanksgiving.

ALMIGHTY God, most high, most holy and supreme, just and holy Father, Lord and King of heaven and earth, we thank Thee for Thyself, for through Thy holy will and Thine only Son and the Holy Spirit Thou hast made all things, both spiritual and material, and having created us in Thine image and likeness, Thou didst place us in paradise, whence by our own fault we have fallen.

We thank Thee that, having made us through Thy Son, Thy true and holy love for us caused Him to be born of the glorious and blessed ever-virgin Mary as true God and true man, and that Thou hast willed that we should be redeemed from our bondage by His Cross, and Blood, and Death.

We thank Thee that Thy Son Himself will return in the glory of His majesty to sentence the wicked, who refuse to repent and have not acknowledged Thee, to everlasting fire, and to say to all who have acknowledged, adored, and served Thee in penitence, *Come, you that have received a blessing from My Father; take possession of the kingdom which has been prepared for you since the foundation of the world.*

And because we are all miserable sinners, unworthy to utter Thy Name, we humbly implore Thee that Thy beloved Son our Lord Jesus Christ, in Whom Thou art well pleased, together with the Holy Paraclete, may offer thanks to Thee for all things in accordance with Thy and Their good pleasure. For He is ever pleasing to Thee in all things, and through Him Thou hast done marvellous things for us. Alleluia.

And for love of Thee we humbly implore the glorious Mother Mary, ever-virgin, blessed Michael, Gabriel, Raphael, and all the choirs of blessed spirits, Seraphim, Cherubim, Thrones, Dominations, Principalities and Powers, Virtues, Angels and Archangels, blessed John the Baptist, Peter, Paul, the blessed Patriarchs, Innocents, Apostles, Evangelists, Disciples, Martyrs, Confessors, Virgins, blessed Elias and Enoch, and all Saints past, present, and to come, to offer our thanks for all these blessings to Thee, the one true God, living and eternal, and to Thy beloved Son our Lord Jesus Christ, and to the Holy Spirit the Paraclete, for ever and ever. *Amen. Alleluia.*

And to all who desire to serve God in the holy, catholic and apostolic Church, all clergy, priests, deacons and subdeacons, acolytes, exorcists, readers, door-keepers, clerks, all monks and nuns, young people and children, poor and needy, kings and princes, labourers, farmers, servants and masters, married and single, laymen and laywomen, babies, boys and girls, youths and maidens, young men and old, healthy and sick, great and small, and to all peoples, races, tribes and languages, all nations, and all throughout the world, both now and in time to come: We, all Friar Minors, *unprofitable servants*, humbly address and appeal to all of you to pray for grace, that we may all persevere in the true Faith and in penitence, for without this none can be saved.

Let us all love the Lord God with all our heart, with all our soul, with all our mind, and with all our strength; with all our understanding and all our powers, with all our effort, with all our feelings and affections, with all our desire and will. For it is He Who gives us our soul, our life, and all things; Who has created and redeemed us, and has saved us solely through His mercy; Who has given and ever gives all good things to us wretched and miserable sinners, corrupt, foul, ungrateful and evil as we are.

Let us therefore desire nothing, wish for nothing, take pleasure and delight in nothing except our Creator, Redeemer, and

Saviour, the one true God, Who is the plenitude of goodness, all good, complete good, the true and supreme good. For He alone is holy, just, true, and righteous; He alone is beneficent, innocent, pure, and from Him, through Him, and in Him is all pardon, all grace, all glory for the penitent and the righteous, as for all the blessed saints who rejoice together in heaven.

Let nothing hinder us, nothing separate us, nothing disturb us. Let us all, everywhere and always, daily and constantly believe in Him sincerely and humbly. Let us enshrine the most high, supreme, eternal God in our hearts; let us honour, adore, praise and bless, glorify and exalt, magnify and thank Him Who is Trinity in Unity, the Father, the Son, and the Holy Spirit, Creator of all things, and the Saviour of all who love, hope, and trust in Him. He is without beginning and without end, immutable, invisible, unutterable, ineffable, incomprehensible, unfathomable. He is worthy of all blessing, praise and glory, exalted, sublime, sweet, lovable, full of delight, and to be desired above all things for ever and ever.

In the Name of the Lord I beg all friars to learn the text and meaning of all that is written in this Rule of life for the salvation of our souls, and to meditate upon it frequently. And I pray God Almighty, Trinity in Unity, to bless all who teach it, learn it, observe it, remember it, and practise it, whenever they recite it and carry out all that is written here for our salvation. And I beg them all, kissing their feet, to love, observe and uphold the Rule. And in the name of Almighty God, of the Lord Pope, and of obedience, I, Brother Francis, strictly enjoin and require that nothing be removed from or added to this Rule of life, and that the friars observe no other.

> Glory be to the Father, and to the Son, and to the Holy Spirit. As it was in the beginning is now, and ever shall be, world without end. *Amen*.

THE SECOND RULE OF THE FRIARS MINOR

The latter years of Saint Francis's life were burdened by a variety of illnesses, which sapped his strength and reduced his activity. As a result he tended increasingly to stand aside from the controversies within the Order, and to withdraw to the more secluded houses for prayer and contemplation. After the brief Generalship of Peter Catanii, control and direction of affairs passed into the capable but worldly hands of Brother Elias and Cardinal Ugolino, who, contrary to Saint Francis's expressed wishes, obtained various privileges for the Order from the Pope.

Despite the concessions granted in the Rule of 1221, a new Rule was called for to meet the conditions and demands prevailing in the Order, and Saint Francis was asked to compile it. During his stay at Fonte Colombo for this purpose, Brother Elias and his supporters called on the Saint and protested that they refused to be bound by a strict Rule, and when the Rule was produced, these Ministers conveniently 'lost' it, so that Saint Francis was compelled to dictate another. He took this last Rule to Rome in order to obtain papal approval, and having prevailed on Saint Francis to modify his insistence on absolute poverty still further, Honorius confirmed the Rule with a Bull dated November 25, 1223. So at last the Franciscan Rule received the formal approval of the Church, but while it retained much of the Saint's original purposes, it was considerably modified and amended. Saint Francis was deeply distressed to find so few of his brethren prepared to follow him in his devotion to poverty, simplicity, and 'the perfect following of the Gospel,' and the Church itself unwilling to admit the practical possibility of such an ideal.

IN THE NAME OF THE LORD. HERE BEGINS THE WAY OF LIFE OF THE FRIARS MINOR

1

THE Rule and way of life of the Friars Minor is this: to observe the holy Gospel of our Lord Jesus Christ by living under obedience, without possessions, and in chastity. Brother Francis promises obedience and reverence to the Lord Pope Honorius and his successors canonically elected, and to the Roman Church. And the other friars shall be bound to obey Brother Francis and his successors.

2

On those who wish to adopt this life, and how they are to be received.

WHENEVER any man wishes to embrace this life and approaches friars on the matter, they are to direct him to their Provincial Ministers, who are the only brethren with authority to admit friars. The Minister shall carefully examine him on the Catholic Faith and the Sacraments of the Church. If he believes all these things and is prepared to profess and observe them faithfully to the end; and if he is not married, or if married, his wife has already entered a convent, or if both parties have agreed to take a vow of continence, and received the approval of the diocesan bishop; or if his wife is of such an age that no cause for scandal can arise; then the Minister may address him in the words of the Holy Gospel, and tell him to go and sell all his possessions and give to the poor. But should circumstances make this impossible for him, his goodwill shall suffice. Both the friars and their Ministers are to avoid interfering in a man's disposal of his property, so that he is free to deal with it as the Lord may move him. But should he ask for guidance, the Minister may send him to some devout person who shall advise him how best to dispose of his goods to the benefit of the poor. This done, if

228

God guides the Minister to accept him, he may be clothed as a postulant; and given two habits without a hood, a cord, and under-garment, and a waist-length cloak. After a year's probation, he shall be allowed to take a vow of obedience and promise to observe this life and Rule. And in accordance with the decree of the Lord Pope, he will on no account be permitted to leave this Order, for the holy Gospel says, *No man who looks behind him, when he has once put his hand to the plough, is fitted for the kingdom of God.* Those who have taken vows of obedience may have a single habit with a hood, and if they need it, another habit without a hood. Those who really need them may wear sandals. All friars are to wear coarse garments, and with God's blessing they may mend them with patches of sacking and suchlike. But I warn them not to despise or condemn other men who wear expensive coloured garments and indulge in choice food and drink; let every friar judge and despise himself.

3

On the Divine Office, fasting, and the behaviour of friars in the world.

WHEN they possess breviaries, clergy will recite the Divine Office according to the use of the holy Roman Church, with the exception of the Psalter. Lay-Brothers will say twenty-four *Our Father's* for Matins; five for Lauds; seven each for Prime, Terce, Sext, and None; twelve for Vespers; seven for Compline; and they will pray for the departed.

The friars are to fast from the Feast of All Saints until Christmass. The fast, hallowed by our Lord's own fast of forty days, which begins at Epiphany is a voluntary observance; God bless those who keep it, but none is obliged to keep it against his will. But all are to fast during Lent until Easter. The friars are not to be obliged to fast at other seasons except on Fridays. In times of great need, however, friars shall not be obliged to fast.

I advise and warn my brothers in the Lord Jesus Christ not to take part in quarrels and controversies or to criticize others when they go about the world. They should be gentle, peaceable and modest, forbearing and humble, speaking honestly to all in a fitting manner. They are not to ride on horseback unless obliged to do so by weakness or by pressing need. And *when they enter a house, let them first say, Peace be to this house.* And, as the holy Gospel allows, friars may eat any food that is set before them.

4

That friars may not accept money.

I STRICTLY forbid all friars to accept money on any account, either themselves or through a third person. But with the help of spiritual friends the Ministers and Guardians shall take care to provide for the needs of the sick and the clothing of the other friars in a manner suited to the locality, the season of the year and the coldness of the country, always provided that they do not receive money.

5

On the work of the friars.

THOSE friars to whom God has given the grace to labour are to do so honestly and devoutly so as to avoid idleness, the enemy of the soul, while not quenching the spirit of prayer and devotion, which must come before all worldly things. In payment for their work they may accept bodily necessities for themselves and their brethren, but not money, and they are to accept what is given them humbly as befits servants of God and observers of most holy poverty.

6

That friars are to have no possessions; on alms; on the care of the sick.

FRIARS are not to acquire any possessions, whether houses, land, or anything whatsoever. They must serve the Lord in humility and poverty, living as *strangers and exiles* in this life. They are to ask alms with confidence, nor need they be ashamed to do so, for our Lord made Himself poor in this world for our sakes. Herein lies the dignity of most noble poverty, which has made you, dearest brothers, heirs and kings of the kingdom of heaven, poor in worldly goods but enriched in virtue. Let poverty be your inheritance, and lead you into the land of the living. Dearest brothers, be completely loyal to poverty, and in the Name of our Lord Jesus Christ have no wish to possess anything under heaven but Him.

When friars happen to meet, they are to show brotherly kindness to one another. Let each have no hesitation in telling the other if he is in need, for if a mother cherishes her own child, how much more should a friar love and cherish one who is his own spiritual brother? And if any friar falls sick, the others are to look after him as they would wish to be cared for themselves.

7

On the penances to be imposed for wrongdoing.

IF any friar succumbs to the promptings of the devil and commits mortal sin, and his brethren consider that the matter can only be dealt with by the Provincial Ministers, the offending friar shall be obliged to present himself before them as soon as possible and without delay. If the Provincial Ministers are themselves priests, they are to impose penance on him with mercy; but if they are not priests, penance is to be imposed by other priests of the Order as the Lord guides them. But let them beware of being angered and disquieted by the wrongdoing of any friars, for anger and disquiet banishes charity both in oneself and in others.

8

On the election of the Minister-General of this Fraternity, and the Whitsun Chapter.

ALL friars are to acknowledge one of the brethren of this Order as Minister-General and servant of the whole Fraternity, and must yield him absolute obedience. At his death the election of his successor shall be effected by the Ministers Provincial and the Guardians at the Whitsun Chapter, when the Ministers Provincial shall be obliged to attend at whatever place the late Minister-General had appointed. This Chapter shall take place at least every three years unless the Minister General shall decide otherwise. If at any time a majority of the Ministers Provincial and Guardians should consider the Minister-General incapable of serving the needs of the brethren, these friars, in whose hands the choice rests, shall in God's Name elect another in his place.

After the Whitsun Chapter all Ministers and Guardians may, if they think it desirable, summon a chapter of friars in their own custodies once during that year.

9

On preachers.

FRIARS are not to preach in the diocese of any bishop who has refused his consent. And no friar shall presume to preach to people unless he has been examined and approved by the Minister-General of this Fraternity and received permission to exercise the office of preacher. I warn and remind friars that whenever they preach their words are to be well chosen and pure, so as to help and edify the people, and to define virtues and vices, punishment and glory. And let them be brief, for the Lord Himself while on earth was brief.

10

On the reproof and correction of the friars.

THOSE who are the Ministers and servants of the other friars shall visit and advise their own brethren. They are to correct them humbly and with love, and must never order them to act contrary to their own conscience or to our Rule. Brethren who are under obedience should remember that they have surrendered their own wills for God's sake. And I strictly charge them to obey their Ministers in all matters that they have promised to observe, and that are not opposed to their consciences or to the Rule. Should friars ever find themselves unable to observe the Rule properly, they may and should seek the advice of their Ministers. And the Ministers are to receive them lovingly and kindly, and show them such friendship that the friars feel free to speak and behave with them as masters with their servants. For this should be the right relationship, since the Ministers are the servants of all the friars.

I warn the friars and beg them in the Name of our Lord Jesus Christ to beware of all pride, boasting, jealousy, and avarice, of the cares and preoccupations of this world, and detraction and complaint against others. Those who do not know how to read need not rush off to learn; instead, let them remember that their chief desire should be to possess the spirit of the Lord and His holy grace, to pray to Him at all times with a pure heart, to remain humble and patient in persecution and hardship, and to love those who persecute, accuse, and blame us. For our Lord says, *Love your enemies, and pray for those who persecute and insult you. Blessed are they who suffer persecution in the cause of right;*

the kingdom of heaven is theirs. And, That man will be saved who endures to the last.

11

That friars shall not enter convents of nuns.

I STRICTLY forbid all friars to have any dealings or conversations with women such as could give rise to gossip. And none but those who have received special permission are to enter convents of nuns. Friars are not permitted to be godfathers of men or women, in order to avoid any scandal arising among the friars or about the friars.

12

On those who go among the Saracens and other unbelievers.

ANY friars who feel called by God to go among the Saracens or other unbelievers are to ask permission from their Provincial Minister. The Provincial Ministers shall only grant permission to those who are clearly suitable to be sent.

I also require the Ministers under obedience to request the Lord Pope to appoint one of the Cardinals of the holy Roman Church to be governor, protector, and corrector of this fraternity. In this way we shall be under discipline and subject at the feet of the same holy Church and firm in the Catholic Faith, and shall observe poverty, humility, and the holy Gospel of our Lord Jesus Christ as we have solemnly vowed.